You see a photograph of the moon's-eye view of the earth and you recognize it immediately. Now, when you stop and think about it, that's mighty strange. A few years ago such a picture was the figment of the imagination of a science fiction writer. Times are changing—and so fast—you can't help but wonder "What's this world coming to?"

Is there anything you can be sure of? Is anything changeless or at least predictable? Where can a man turn these days to get a trustworthy view of where he stands in this unfolding drama of time? There is a place! Jesus Christ told about your tomorrows a long time ago and what he said is written for you to read. This book discusses his words.

"What's this world coming to?"

Read on and find out!

Ray C. Stedman

WHAT'S THIS WORLD COMING TO?

AN EXPOSITORY STUDY OF MATTHEW 24-25
THE OLIVET DISCOURSE

Regal Books
A Division of GL Publications
Ventura, California, U.S.A.

Rights for publishing this book in other languages are contracted by Gospel Literature International (GLINT) foundation. GLINT also provides technical help for the adaptation, translation, and publishing of Bible study resources and books in scores of languages worldwide. For further information, contact GLINT, Post Office Box 6688, Ventura, California 93006, U.S.A., or the publisher.

Second Edition, First Printing, 1986
Formerly published under the title *What On Earth's Going to Happen?*

Published by Regal Books
A Division of GL Publications
Ventura, California 93006
Printed in U.S.A.

Library of Congress Cataloging in Publication Data

Stedman, Ray C.
    What's this world coming to?

    Rev. ed. of: What on earth's going to happen? 1970.
    1. Bible. N.T. Matthew XXIV-XXV—Prophecies.
I. Stedman, Ray C. What on earth's going to happen? II. Title.
BS647.2.S66   1986   226′.206   86-6439
ISBN 0-8307-1154-6

1 2 3 4 5 6 7 8 9 10 / 91 90 89 88 87 86

CONTENTS

The Long Look Ahead
Matthew 24:1-3

How would you like to know the future? Who does not want to lift, if possible, the curtain that hides the things to come, and read the future as well as he can the past? Many are trying it today with varying degrees of success, but the only book with a batting average of 1.000 is the Bible. That's one of the things that makes it such a fascinating book. It is always up-to-date and filled with the most pertinent, often exciting information. In fact, it is more than up-to-date—it is ahead of the times.

There are many predictive passages in both Old and New Testaments, but none is clearer or more detailed than the message delivered by Jesus himself as he sat on the Mount of Olives overlooking the city of Jerusalem during the turbulent events of his last week before the cross. These words have immense significance for us for they are a revelation of the ultimate fate of earth. From his point in time (about A.D. 32*) he looks ahead to foretell the destruction of the city of Jerusalem and the disturbances connected with that singular event. He looks on across the centuries and outlines the perils that lie between his first and

---

*According to the calculations of Sir Robert Anderson, *The Coming Prince*, Hodder and Stoughton, 1909.

second coming, thus describing the very age in which we live. He looks past the present day to that time which he calls "the end of the age" and sets its events before us in searing and vivid detail, culminating in his own return to earth and the ushering in of a new day.

Unfolding events

As we read his perceptive words we shall discover that what is coming is but the unfolding of events which will grow out of movements and processes already at work in human society. The future has already begun, and our Lord's outlining of its course will greatly help us to understand what is taking place in our own day. In this first chapter we shall look only at three verses which introduce Christ's amazing message to us and provide for us the key to its structure and the events out of which it came. They are the first three verses of Matthew 24:

> "Jesus left the temple and was going away, when his disciples came to point out to him the buildings of the temple. But he answered them, 'You see all these, do you not? Truly, I say to you, there will not be left here one stone upon another, that will not be thrown down.'"
>
> "As he sat on the Mount of Olives, the disciples came to him privately, saying, 'Tell us, when will this be, and what will be the sign of your coming and of the close of the age?'"

It sounds strange to us that the disciples should come to Jesus at this time and point out to him the beauty of the Temple buildings. He had often seen the Temple and the disciples had frequently been with him as he taught in its courts. Why then this sudden interest in the buildings? It all grew out of the astonishment of these disciples at the recent actions of the Lord. The chapter opens with the pregnant phrase, "Jesus left the temple." When he left the Temple on this occasion he never entered it again. He left it after having pronounced upon it a sentence of judgment, recorded in the closing words of chapter 23:

> "O Jerusalem, Jerusalem, killing the prophets and stoning those who are sent to you! How often would I have gathered your children together as a hen gathers her brood under her wings, and you would not! Behold, your house [the Temple] is forsaken and desolate. For I tell you, you will not see me again, until you say, 'Blessed is he who comes in the name of the Lord.'"

All of this comes at the close of the most blistering sermon he ever delivered. It was addressed to the scribes and the Pharisees, and consisted of a series of "woes" pronounced upon the hypocrisy of these religious leaders. They were supposed to be the teachers of the people but were actually hindering them from knowing the truth of God. Jesus began his ministry with a series of eight blessings (the Beatitudes, Matthew 5), and he ended it with a series of eight woes.

Nothing arouses more vehement anger in the heart of God than religious hypocrisy. Throughout the Scriptures, God's most scorching terms are reserved for those who profess to know him but who behave quite contrary to their profession— especially for the self-righteous.

Cleansing the Temple

Having completed this sermon, Jesus, for the second time, cleansed the Temple of the money changers. John records the first occasion (2:13-21) which occurred at the beginning of the Lord's ministry. Many do not realize that he did this twice, but Mark records that when he came to Jerusalem for the last week,

9

he went into the Temple and began to drive out those who bought and sold. Further, Mark records a most significant action of our Lord's. Mark says, "he would not allow any one to carry anything through the temple" (Mark 11:16).

This strongly suggests that he stopped the priests who bore vessels through the Temple in order to bring the blood of the sacrifices offered in the outer court into the holy place where it was to be sprinkled before the altar. Jesus arrested this procession. He brought to a close, for the first time since the days of the Maccabees, the offerings of Israel. They were later resumed by the Jews but without meaning or divine sanction. When Jesus himself became upon the cross "the Lamb of God which takes away the sins of the world," he thereby declared all other sacrifice as no longer of any meaning or value.

Then, having stopped the sacrifices, the next day the Lord stood in quiet dignity and pronounced the official sentence of rejection, "Behold, your house is forsaken and desolate. For I tell you, you will not see me again, until you say, 'Blessed is he who comes in the name of the Lord.'" Having said this he left the Temple and the disciples went with him. Silently, they walked down through the valley of the Kidron and up the other side to the Mount of Olives. There Jesus took his seat upon one of the rocks that overlooked the city and the Temple area. The disciples were troubled and confused. They could not understand his actions or his words concerning the Temple. The Temple was the center of the nation's life and they regarded it with holy awe as the very dwelling place of God among his people. Its beauty was famous throughout the earth and they could not believe that God would allow any harm to come to it. So they began to point out to Jesus the strength and beauty of the Temple.

To this he responds with words which distress them even further: "Truly, I say to you, there will not be left here one stone upon another, that will not be thrown down." They cannot believe that this will happen. They knew, of course, that the nation was under the bondage of Rome. They had no final authority in their own city or land. But it was well known that the Romans were lovers of temples. It was their boast that they preserved, if at all possible, the temples and monuments of any country they conquered. They had been in power in Palestine for many years and they had not destroyed the Temple. There seemed no good reason, therefore, why this Temple should ever be destroyed. But Jesus solemnly assures them that there would not be one stone left standing upon another.

Test of a prophet

We shall surely miss the full meaning of this sentence if we fail to see that Jesus is giving here his credentials as a prophet. The law of Moses required that whenever a prophet essayed to foretell the future it was necessary that he give a sign by which his prophecy could be tested. That requirement is found in Deuteronomy 18. In the midst of a prophecy concerning the coming of the Messiah, Moses said, "The Lord your God will raise up for you a prophet like me from among you, from your brethren—him you shall heed." Then, a little later, he quoted God as saying:

> "I will raise up for them a prophet like you from among their brethren; and I will put my words in his mouth, and he shall speak to them all that I command him. And whoever will not give heed to my words which he shall speak in my name, I myself will require it of him" (Deuteronomy 18: 18,19).

Many Bible scholars agree that this was a foreview of the coming of Jesus Christ. He was that prophet, raised up by God among the people of Israel, who would be like Moses and would speak words that the nation should hear. But to mark the authenticity of that prophet, Moses went on to say:

11

"'. . . but the prophet who presumes to speak a word in my name which I have not commanded him to speak, or who speaks in the name of other gods, that same prophet shall die.' And if you say in your heart, 'How may we know the word which the LORD has not spoken?'—when a prophet speaks in the name of the LORD, if the word does not come to pass or come true, that is a word which the LORD has not spoken; the prophet has spoken it presumptuously, you need not be afraid of him" (vv. 20-22).

In the practical carrying out of that admonition it became customary for the prophets to give the people a prediction of something that would occur in the near future. When it came to pass as foretold, the people would know that this was indeed an authenticated prophet. But if the sign did not occur as predicted, the prophecy in its entirety was to be rejected as not from God, and the prophet was exposed as false. So Jesus predicts the downfall of the Temple in the near future as a sign that all else he includes in this discourse is true. This is what lay behind the request of the disciples for a sign associated with his coming.

Prophecy fulfilled

In Luke 21:20 we have other details of this predicted overthrow of the city and the Temple. There Jesus adds, "But when you see Jerusalem surrounded by armies, then know that its desolation has come near." Forty years later the Roman armies under Titus came in and fulfilled the prediction to the very letter. With Titus was a Jewish historian named Josephus who recorded the terrible story in minute detail. It was one of the most ghastly sieges in all history. When the Romans came the city was divided among three warring factions of Jews who were so at each others' throats that they paid no heed to the approach of the Romans. Thus Titus came up and surrounded the city while it was distracted by its own internecine warfare. The Romans assaulted the walls again and again, and gave every opportunity to the Jews to surrender and save their capital from destruction.

During the long siege a terrible famine raged in the city and the bodies of the inhabitants were literally stacked like cordwood in the streets. Mothers ate their children to preserve their own strength. The toll of Jewish suffering was horrible but they would not surrender the city. Again and again they attempted to trick the Romans through guile and perfidy. When at last the walls were breached Titus tried to preserve the Temple by giving orders to his soldiers not to destroy or burn it. But the anger of the soldiers against the Jews was so intense that, maddened by the resistance they encountered, they disobeyed the order of their general and set fire to the Temple. There were great quantities of gold and silver there which had been placed in the Temple for safekeeping. This melted and ran down between the rocks and into the cracks of the stones. When the soldiers captured the Temple area, in their greed to obtain this gold and silver they took long bars and pried apart the massive stones. Thus, quite literally, not one stone was left standing upon another. The Temple itself was totally destroyed, though the wall supporting the area upon which the Temple was built was left partially intact and a portion of it remains to this day, called the Western Wall.

In this remarkable fulfillment, confirmed so strongly by secular history, is convincing proof that God will fulfill every other part of this amazing message fully as literally. As the Lord himself said in the discourse, "Heaven and earth will pass away, but my words will not pass away." With the certainty of its fulfillment underscored so strongly, let us now note the clue to the structure of the discourse, as given in these opening verses.

Three tough questions

There are actually three questions which the disciples ask

13

the Lord. The first is, "Tell us, when will this be?" They mean, of course, the destruction of the Temple. As we have already seen, the answer is recorded by Luke. It would be when they saw Jerusalem surrounded by armies. A number of them were still living when Titus fulfilled the prediction.

The second question is, "What will be the sign of your coming?" The third is, "[What will be the sign] of the close of the age?" These questions are perfectly natural in view of the instruction of Moses to ask for a sign when prediction is attempted. Without doubt there is a great deal of difference between what the disciples had in mind when they asked these questions and what we are thinking of when we read them. They asked out of confusion. There were many things they could not see, or would not believe, and so their questions were difficult to answer. They were much like the little boy who asked his father: "Daddy, why does the sun shine in the daytime when we don't need it, and not at night when we do?" That kind of question is difficult to answer, not because the answer is so hard, but because the question is so wrong. To some degree, that was the problem here.

In many ways we can understand much better than they what their questions meant, for we have the history of twenty centuries to look back upon. Also, we accept the importance of Christ's death and resurrection, against which they were in revolt. Therefore, they could not understand all that he said to them. He had been puzzling them for months and they were now quite out of harmony with him. He had told them plainly of his coming death and resurrection, but they refused to give heed. Since they would not allow themselves to face the terrible specter of his death, they could not have any clear idea of what he meant when he said he was coming again.

The presence of the King

Thus, when they asked him about his coming they did not

14

have in mind a second advent. They did not picture a descent from heaven to earth, nor anything at all of what we mean when we speak of Christ's second coming. They had in mind a political revolution and the crowning of Jesus as King and his subsequent presence among the nation as its acknowledged King and Messiah. They used a very interesting word for coming. It is the Greek word, "parousia." This word appears four times in this passage, in verses 3, 27, 37, and 39. It is not the usual word for coming. It means more than the mere arrival of some person; it also implies his continuing presence after he arrives. This is important, for much of the understanding of this discourse will turn upon the meaning of this word. The English word "coming" appears other times in the message, but it is not the same Greek word and has a different meaning.

Even after the resurrection these disciples were still asking Jesus questions that reflected a political concept of his coming. In Acts 1:6 they asked, "Lord, will you at this time restore the kingdom to Israel?" They were obviously still thinking of a political rule over the nations of earth. He did not deny that this eventually will occur, but simply reminded them that the times and seasons are the Father's prerogative to determine. Thus when they ask him on the Mount of Olives, "What will be the sign of your coming?" it is not a question about his coming again, but of his presence in the nation as its king. But, as we shall see in our Lord's answer, he treats it as a legitimate inquiry concerning his second advent.

The close of the age

They also ask for a second sign, concerning the close of the age. It is not, as in the King James Version, "the end of the world." It has nothing to do with the end of the world. The world will go on for a long time after the events of the Olivet Discourse are fulfilled, but the age will end with those events. In this matter they were much more clearly informed, though they unquestionably felt that it was a time that lay immediately ahead. They were sure that they were living in days approaching the end of the age and that they were about to enter the events that would mark the close of the age.

We must remember that these men were well acquainted with the Old Testament. They also had heard Jesus teaching the parables of the kingdom (Matthew 13) and had heard him speak of a "close of the age" when he would send his angels throughout the earth to gather men to judgment. They knew the Old Testament predictions of Messiah's rule and reign over the earth. Doubtless they knew, too, of Daniel's remarkable prophecy (Daniel 9) that there would be a period of 490 years (seventy weeks of years, or 490 years) from the rebuilding of Jerusalem after the Babylonian captivity until the time of Messiah the Prince. From that prophecy they may well have known that the 490 years were almost completely expired, and it was little wonder that they expected the close of the age to be very near indeed.

A hidden valley of time

What they could not see and could not be expected to see was that there would occur a wide valley of time between the hour in which they asked their question and the close of the age in the far distant future. We cannot blame them for this, for it is difficult to distinguish the two comings of Jesus in the Old Testament prophecies. Peter wrote that the prophets foresaw "the sufferings of Christ and the subsequent glory." But to them it seemed as if they were one great event. What looked to them to be one great mountain range of fulfillment was actually two widely separated ranges with a great valley of time in between.

For instance, in Isaiah 9 there is the well known prediction of a coming child. "For to us a child is born, to us a son is given." That is a prophecy of our Lord's first advent as a baby in Bethlehem. But the rest of the verse says, "and the government will

16

be upon his shoulder, and his name will be called 'Wonderful Counselor, Mighty God, Everlasting Father, Prince of Peace.'" That is clearly referring to his reign in the days of the kingdom which would cover the earth. It will not be fulfilled until the Lord returns to earth again, but these two events are brought together into one verse with no hint of any intervening time.

The sign of the end of the age

The Lord now takes their questions and in answering them reverses the order. They asked about the sign of his presence and the sign of the end of the age. He answers the last one first. The sign of the close of the age is found in verse 15, "the desolating sacrilege . . . standing in the holy place." We shall examine that much more fully later on. The sign of his coming is given in verse 30, "then will appear the sign of the Son of man in heaven." This, too, we shall examine in detail in due course, but throughout this whole passage the Lord takes pains to make clear to his disciples that the end of the age lies far in the distant future.

Here in this great prediction are illustrated two great principles of prophetic fulfillment. First, there is often an unspecified interval of time which may operate to delay final fulfillment far beyond what may otherwise be expected. Jesus warned in Acts 1 that "the times and the seasons [are] not for you to know," but remain always in the Father's sovereign choice. The second principle is that of double fulfillment. When Jesus predicted the encirclement of Jerusalem by hostile armies and its conquest and overthrow, it was fulfilled to the letter less than forty years later. But that historic fulfillment became in turn a preview of another day in the far distant future when again Jerusalem would be surrounded by armies and would face its hour of destruction on a greater scale than ever before. Then it will be the close of the age. The age which is thus to be closed is the age in which we now live.

Predictive certainty

Notice that Jesus speaks to these men as though they would live to see all the events he predicts. Obviously, therefore, he is speaking to them as representative men. Some of them saw the destruction of Jerusalem as he had foretold it, but none would live to see the close of the age, and none would pass through the Great Tribulation. They were uniquely representative men. They were representatives both of Israel and the church. At the time he spoke to them they were Jewish believers, men of Israel, all of them. As such they represented the nation and God's dealings with that remarkable people. But after the cross and Pentecost they were Christians, part of the church, neither Jew nor Greek. They would then belong to a unique body which has a task to fulfill throughout the intervening centuries before the end times. Thus this message includes truth for the church in its relationship to the present age, and also truth for Israel in its time of trouble to come at the end of the age. These disciples are representatives of both groups and our Lord speaks to them as such.

As Jesus sits looking out over the city he is facing the darkest hour of his life. He knows the scheming of his enemies and the opposition that even then is sharpening against him from almost every quarter. He knows what Judas is planning. His enemies think they are doing their nefarious deeds in secret, but he knows it all. He knows the frailty of his friends and that he can never depend upon them. These very disciples who cluster around him on the mountain will in but a few hours forsake him and flee. One of them will even deny him with curses. He knows all that. He sees the darkness of the coming centuries but he looks on through them to the light beyond. When all around him seems utterly hopeless he quietly declares what the end will be, without the slightest uncertainty or doubt.

Our part in history

All things, he says, all events, will find their significance and meaning only in relationship to him. Any event which is not related to his purpose in the age is worthless and useless, without real meaning or significance. As we listen to his declaration of what the course of human history will be, we must each face the inevitable question: In what way is my life related to the great events which Jesus says will take place? Am I contributing to what will ultimately eventuate in anarchy and distress among men and in the failing of hearts for fear of what is coming to pass? Or am I contributing to the program of God which is moving through history to bring the age to its appointed climax and to bring again from heaven the Son of God to establish his kingdom over the earth? It is one or the other.

We do not live in an isolated segment of time. What is happening today in the affairs and councils of men is bringing to pass what our Lord says will occur. We can often trace the connection if we see the events of our day in the light of what he says in this discourse. The great and supreme question is not, what shall I do with my life, or what can I make of it, but, how, does it relate to what God is doing? When God is through with history, this is the way it will be. What part will I have played in the process? These are the questions this Olivet Discourse forces upon us.

Prayer: Father, as we come to this great prophecy we ask for understanding hearts and ears that are ready to hear. Teach us to see that all this is woven into the warp and woof of our lives and that we cannot escape being part of your program. Keep us from being frightened or resentful or bitter or indifferent, but grant that we may be ready to walk in fellowship with you, our Living Lord. In Jesus' name, Amen.

2

The Age of Confusion
Matthew 24:4-14

"What will be the sign of your coming and [the sign] of the close of the age?" This is the question the disciples ask Jesus as he sits on the Mount of Olives with the faithless city spread out below him. We have noted already that the question is not very well put. Their concept of his coming is not at all clear, and they think that the close of the age is perhaps only a few years away. Therefore, the answer Jesus gives is at first seemingly evasive or at least indirect. Matthew says. "And Jesus answered them, 'Take heed that no one leads you astray.'"

The big point—don't be fooled!

In our understandable haste to come to the great events he predicts for the future, let us not miss the heavy emphasis he makes in this opening word. It is the dominant note of this whole discourse. The age will be a time of great uncertainty as to the meaning of events. It will be frightfully easy to misinterpret and therefore to be misled. The phrase "lead astray" forms the structure around which the whole message is built. He used it again in verse 5, "For many will come in my name, saying, 'I am the Christ,' and they will lead many astray." And again in verse 11, "And many false prophets will arise and lead many astray." Once again in verse 24, "For false Christs and false prophets will arise and show great signs and wonders, so as to lead astray, if possible, even the elect."

Because of this continuing possibility, the Lord's exhortation throughout the message is, "Watch!", i.e., keep your eyes open. Evaluate! Test! Try the spirits! Bring everything to the test that you might understand the true character of movements and pressures, for the predominant note of the age will be one of deceit and confusion. Then he proceeds to show to these men that they are already confused in thinking that the end of the age lies immediately ahead. From verse 5 through verse 14 he clearly indicates that there would be a rather long, indeterminate period before the end of the age would begin. These men knew from the prophet Daniel that the end of the age would not be a single spectacular event but a series of events, covering several years. The Lord now begins carefully to trace the age which they could not see, the parenthesis of time in which we also live.

The preliminaries

If we note carefully the time phrases he employs to lead up to the answer to the disciples' question we shall have no difficulty with this section. He is most emphatically not giving so-called "signs of the times" here. To the contrary, he repeatedly indicates that he is tracing a series of events which would appear throughout the age. For instance, he says in verse 6, "And you will hear of wars and rumors of wars; see that you are not alarmed; for this must take place, but the end is not yet." Therefore, despite the commentators who insist that "wars and rumors of wars" are a sign of the near approach of the end, our Lord says quite otherwise. In verse 8, he adds, "all this is but the beginning of the sufferings." He is saying, in effect, "These events are but leading up to the end of the age about which you are asking." Then, finally, in verse 14, after listing a long series of events, he says, " . . . and then the end will come." It is at this point that he at last begins to answer directly the disciples' question, "What will be the sign . . . of the close of the age?" From verse 15 through verse 31 he gives in detail the events that will occur during the end-of-the-age period.

Danger ahead

How then shall we characterize these events he outlines which are to occur in the intervening time before the end of the age is reached? They are of enormous importance to us for we live in this time before the end. If, as we have seen, the dominant note of this discourse is to warn against the allure of the false, the glamour of the phony, and to indicate the ease by which the uninformed may be led astray, then it is immediately evident that in these intervening events he is listing the perils of the age. These are the threats to faith, the powerful forces by which men and women, observing the events of their day, may be misled into confusion and error. These perils to faith are forces, deceptive in their character, which will mislead men throughout the whole course of this intervening time. They make it difficult to believe, they act powerfully upon men's minds to turn them from the unseen spiritual kingdom to depend only upon the things of sense and time. Each peril, when once introduced, runs on to the end of the age.

The first peril—phony christs

Let us now examine these perils one by one. The first, in verse 5, is the peril of the counterfeit, "For many will come in my name, saying, 'I am the Christ,' and they will lead many astray." The apostle John wrote at the close of the first century,

"For many [antichrists] have gone out into the world." The term "antichrist" does not indicate someone who is openly against Christ, like an atheist or a pagan. Rather it is one who appears instead of Christ, and in this sense opposes true Christianity. It is a counterfeit Christ.

Of course it includes the originators or propagators of all the false cults which have arisen throughout the course of the age, beginning with the first century. We have witnessed the rise of many in the last few decades, especially those with the label, "Made in America," like Jehovah's Witnesses, Mormonism, Christian Science, Moonieism, Scientology and others. These are outwardly Christian in language and activity but their basic message is antichristian, rejecting the true Christ. Any person or organization which purports to be Christian in its outward aspects, but whose message is actually opposed to Christian faith is an antichrist. It is the rise of these groups which our Lord predicts. What a peril to faith they have proved to be.

But by no means are these the most deceptive of the antichristian voices. Perhaps our Lord is thinking of even subtler expressions. We will miss the full meaning of his words if we look only for those who actually say, "I am the Messiah," or "We have the true Christian message." Are they not more dangerous who claim to do what only Jesus Christ alone can really do? "I am the Way," says that lonely Man who died forsaken upon the cross. "We are the way," say all the many voices that attract today: politics, patriotism, social work, literacy crusades. These are often really fine works, but when they claim to meet the basic problem of human life, they become antichristian. Their claim is false, and many are deceived throughout the course of the age. They offer to lead men into peace without forgiveness, and thus are really evil masquerading as angels of light. How many are being misled by these siren voices which neglect the narrow way by which an individual is confronted with the person of Jesus Christ—the one way to redemption and cleansing and forgiveness of sin?

The second peril—conflict

The second peril Jesus foresees is that of conflict. "And you will hear of wars and rumors of wars; see that you are not alarmed; for this must take place, but the end is not yet. For nation will rise against nation, and kingdom against kingdom." Clearly he is not here predicting any one specific war or revolution. He is characterizing the general course of the age. It will be marked by continual turmoil among nations, and the fears, the alarms, the degradation, the horror, the misery of war. His words telescope together all the effect that wars produce on the human heart.

What a threat to faith war is! Many a young man has been deceived by the glory of war and has left home to march proudly away. But in the carnage and slaughter of battle his eyes have been opened. He has come home, disillusioned, sickened by it all, and must continually fight bitterness and despair. That is the deceitfulness of war. Many will remember the horror of the mushroom cloud hanging over Hiroshima, the scream of air-raid sirens and the terrible challenge to faith those events produced. How many have lost all the flickering of faith in bitter resentment against the wars in Viet Nam or Korea?

The third peril—natural calamity

Another peril Jesus foresees is natural calamity. "And there will be famines and earthquakes in various places: all this is but the beginning of the sufferings." For almost two thousand years these natural calamities have been occurring. They are not, therefore, "signs of the times." Jesus simply states that during the intervening age there will be famines, pestilences, earthquakes, and other natural disasters, and each one will be a threat to belief in God. Sometimes Christians mistakenly try to convince skeptics that God is love by parading the evidences of nature. They describe the beauty of the sunset, the glory of the mountains, the abundant provision in the natural world for the needs of man. But what becomes of that argument when typhoons rage and floods rise and sweep away houses and whole cities are destroyed? What does one say when tornados and earthquakes bury one's children in their ruins, and famine takes the bread from their lips, and parents must watch their children's swollen, distended bodies, with no food to give them? Where, then, is the argument for the love of God as revealed in nature?

How do you preach God's love to those who are stumbling along in dumb terror, fleeing the horror of a volcano which is belching out smoking ashes and burying their homes and cities? Who has not felt the shivers of doubt that come when we read of terrible disasters caused by natural calamities and must square them somehow with our concept of a God who rules and reigns in the midst of all human events? Granted, such doubt can be answered by a clearer understanding of the purposes and workings of God, but how many are pressured by grief to believe the apparently obvious and will not wait for an explanation? Surely we need our Lord's warning, "Take heed that no one leads you astray."

The fourth peril—persecution

Another terrible threat to faith appears in verse 9, "Then they will deliver you up to tribulation, and put you to death; and you will be hated by all nations for my name's sake." Here the peril is religious persecution. This began shortly after the day of Pentecost when Stephen and James were slain and the disciples were scattered. Who is not familiar with the terrible stories of Christians who were thrown to lions, burned as human torches, mangled by wild beasts, killed by gladiators, tortured, torn apart by wild horses, or martyred in other dreadful ways? Another great period of martyrdom broke out at the time of the Reformation in the 16th and 17th centuries. We can read the gruesome accounts in *Fox's Book of Martyrs*.

But do you know what is the most tortuous century of all? The century in which more Christians have died for their faith than in any other is the 20th century! It is estimated that more Christians were tortured and slain in twelve months during World War II than died under Rome in all the early centuries. In the city of Seoul, Korea, ten thousand Christians have already suffered martyrdom for their faith. Some authorities claim that over fifteen million Christians have been slaughtered in Russia, Soviet-controlled Europe, and other Communist countries. Since Christianity began, no generation has seen such world-wide persecution as is now in progress.

We can scarcely realize the cost of discipleship in certain parts of the world. Recently a Christian magazine contained the account of a young Arab who had turned from Islam to Christ. The magazine told his story only because it could add in a foot-note, "His body now lies buried on a hillside in his own native land. (He was slain by his own relatives.) We can now print his testimony because he can no longer suffer recrimination for it."

Ask yourself, how many have wanted to be Christians, have heard the message, have been drawn to Christ by the preaching of the good news, but have taken a long look at the price they must pay in terms of misunderstanding, exclusion and ridicule, and have quietly melted back into the crowd? Jesus spoke of seed that would fall on shallow ground and spring up, but when the sun came out in burning heat, it would wither and die. How many in America would disappear from our churches if persecution began to break out? What an enemy to faith it is. How the heart trembles and quivers before the thought of torture, or sometimes even of misunderstanding!

The fifth peril—apostasy

Then the Lord put his finger squarely upon another peril to faith. "And then many will fall away, and betray one another, and hate one another." This is the terrible pressure of apostasy.

When combined with persecution it represents a powerful double attack upon a quiet trust in Christ. It is highly disturbing to be left standing alone; to see, one by one, those who previously were on your side, depart, give in, succumb to the pressure and leave you unsupported and alone. If they also betray you in the process, it is almost unbearable. "Demas . . . has [forsaken] me, [having loved] this present world," writes the apostle Paul from his cold prison in Rome. Even to such a doughty spirit as his, that must have been a severe blow. What young person today does not feel the pressure of the world's sneering contempt for sexual and social standards that were once held by almost all? How many have thus "fallen away," driven by the spread of a philosophy of moral relativism that teaches that only the situation can determine whether a thing is bad or good? And when such folly is openly advocated by leaders of the church, who can help but feel his faith tremble a bit?

The sixth peril—cynicism

In close connection with this Jesus adds, "And many false prophets will arise and lead many astray. And because wickedness is multiplied, most men's love will grow cold." Here the peril is cynicism. It is a cold and brutal indifference which arises out of the teaching of "false prophets." Do not read this as though these are religious men, necessarily. The false Christs the Lord had mentioned earlier were unquestionably religious, but here he uses the term "prophet." It refers to any who speak authoritatively—philosophers, professors, scientists, statesmen—those leaders of thought who shape and mold the thinking of the common man. What they will teach is the sanctity of self-interest, the insistence on having "my rights" no matter what happens to the other fellow. The true prophet insists on the rights of God, but the false prophet upholds only the rights of man. Jesus predicts that a tragic and inevitable sequence will follow. First, many will be led astray by the false teaching of the leaders of thought; "because [of this], wickedness [will be] multiplied" (the Greek word used here for wickedness is "anomia," lawlessness); and the result of lawlessness is, "most men's love will grow cold."

One needs only to read the daily papers to see how true this is. The overthrow of moral limits always destroys the fire and glow of love. The psychologists and philosophers who seek to measure the pulse of our times tell us that the major problem of our age is meaninglessness—the loss of fire in life, the coldness of the human heart. Since men cannot live without fire they replace true love with the false fire of lust, and its inevitable consequence, hate. Watch those who feel they can, with impunity, step over the moral bounds of the past. See how they grow hard and callous and cynical. Life becomes for them an increasing tangle of emptiness.

There seems little reason to doubt that here is the explanation for the rocketing divorce rates of our day and for the rapidly increasing frequency of sex crimes and crimes of violence. Often these are accompanied by moral apathy and callous indifference to cruelty. Only recently the papers reported the cases of two mothers who lost all natural affection. One threw her baby in the path of a truck, and the other left hers on a dump heap. How true these words are: "because wickedness is multiplied . . . love . . . grow[s] cold."

Anti-Christian currents

Here are the clanging gongs that Jesus says will sound throughout the age, to drown if they can the still, small voice of faith. He warns against the perils of counterfeit faith, of human conflict, of natural calamity, of religious persecution, of growing apostasy, and callous cynicism. These are the sweeping, powerful currents that will flow throughout the age, gathering as a vast and resistless flood of deceit; distorting, twisting, deluding, so that men are deceived and misled and the whole race is at last

28

swept along over the brink of destruction into the black and raging waters of the world's last day.

How can anyone resist this? Who is equal to these pressures? Who has the wisdom to distinguish the truth from error in these powerful voices? Who can point out the way of faith when these things are happening?

The power to stand

Fortunately for us, Jesus does not stop with this black picture. He goes on to a further unveiling. It is of enormous importance, for it contains the secret of power—the power to stand against deceit and delusion and to avoid the fate of being "led astray." It is introduced by that corner word, "but."

"But he who endures to the end will be saved. And this gospel of the kingdom will be preached throughout the whole world, as a testimony to all nations; and then the end will come."

Despite the pressures, despite the impossibility of the natural mind's remaining undeceived, despite the subtle siren voices that sound—nevertheless, some will see through the distortions, the perversions of truth, the silken deceptions, and will stand true. Some will endure to the end. These will not and cannot be overthrown. They will be saved. The first end referred to here is not the end of the age, for obviously, no one could live through the entire twenty centuries of this intervening age. What Jesus means here is the end of life. These words of Jesus are often distorted to mean that if someone does his best to hang on and live a good clean life, then, if he endures to the end he will be saved. But it is quite the other way around. If he is truly saved, then he will endure to the end and the fact that he so endures makes obvious to all that he is saved.

No doubt it is true that there is no use having a good beginning if there is not a strong finish; but it is equally true that there is no possibility of a strong finish unless there has been a good beginning. Only those who have genuinely found Christ will endure to the end. What our Lord is bringing out here is that the strength of character which permits them to stand fast demands an unceasing flow of power, for they are exposed to an unceasing flow of pressure. They can stand only if there is a power available that can keep them every single moment of the way.

Not just standing, but speaking!

That power is revealed in what these people say. They will not only stand, but they will speak as well. "This gospel of the kingdom," Jesus said, "will be preached throughout the whole world, as a testimony to all nations." The good news they preach reveals the secret of their ability to stand. They tell everywhere the story of One who "has delivered us from the dominion of darkness and transferred us to the kingdom of his beloved Son" (Colossians 1:13). Amid the pressures of the age they reveal that they have heard and obeyed the good news, and there stands with them One whose very life is imparted to them and who can keep them against all the deceit of the world in which they live.

It was the Lord himself who said, "My sheep hear my voice, and I know them, and they follow me." No matter how the wolves howl, fangs drip, and opposition mounts on every side, still they will follow him. Why? Because, as he goes on to say, "I give them eternal life; and they shall never perish, and no one shall snatch them out of my hand. My Father, who has given them to me, is greater than all, and no one is able to snatch them out of the Father's hand." This is what keeps them and makes them able to stand in the midst of a flood of deceit. They will move against the stream, sometimes in blood and tears and terrible loneliness, but they will not succumb.

One unmistakable sign

When this good news of "the kingdom of his beloved Son"

has been preached as a testimony to all nations, then shall the end of the age begin, said Jesus. That is one unmistakable mark of the approaching end. It is supremely significant that this present generation is the first generation in twenty long centuries of which it may be unreservedly said that the gospel is being preached throughout the whole world to all nations. This is properly a "sign of the times" which marks the near approach of the end. When the sirens of the Last Day begin to moan, and the panicky, jostling crowd tries to get in the door at the last moment, then will be unveiled the deceitfulness of the age. But only those who have learned to walk day by day will be able to endure to the end.

In the light of this clear revelation of the character of the age, the exhortation of Jesus takes on new impact. "Watch," he said, "for you do not know on what day your Lord is coming." The question he leaves with us is: What is there in your life that is different from another's? Do not prate about outward religious differences. They do not count. They can all too easily be a part of the "broad way that leads to destruction." Have you stood at the narrow way and done business with the One who says truly, "I am the way, and the truth, and the life."? Is his life in you? Has he come to indwell you, to strengthen and keep you every day by a continual impartation of his life through you, in terms of your personality? This alone will make the difference. The test of reality is endurance, and only those who thus stand have ever really known him.

Prayer: Father, how confusing are the voices we hear; how accurate is our Lord's prediction that these voices will be sounding out in ever increasing clamor to deceive us, mislead us, pervert and destroy us. How thankful we are for that other voice, the clear voice of the Holy Spirit who interprets to us the truth of Scripture. Help us to ask him to begin his wonderful work of sustaining and keeping, empowering and strengthening, till we can stand in the midst of the flood of deceit around us. In Jesus' name, Amen.

3

The Worship of Man
Matthew 24:15-22

"Then shall the end come." With these dramatic words, Jesus begins to answer the question of the disciples, "What will be the sign of . . . the close of the age?" He has prefaced these words with a powerful telescopic view which sweeps through all the intervening centuries and describes their character as one of deception and confusion. Now he focuses upon the (to the disciples) far-distant period which he calls, "the end of the age." Without further delay he describes, in Matthew 24:15-22, the sign of the close of the age:

> "So when you see the desolating sacrilege spoken of by the prophet Daniel, standing in the holy place (let the reader understand), then let those who are in Judea flee to the mountains; let him who is on the housetop not go down to take what is in his house; and let him who is in the field not turn back to take his mantle. And alas for those who are with child and for those who give suck in those days! Pray

that your flight may not be in winter or on a sabbath. For then there will be great tribulation, such as has not been from the beginning of the world until now, no, and never will be. And if those days had not been shortened, no human being would be saved; but for the sake of the elect those days will be shortened."

Unprecedented trouble

The Lord's language here is the most somber he could employ. He is speaking of a time of trouble that is coming, the like of which has never been seen before in all history. It will be a time of superlative distress, of unprecedented peril to human life, a time of shattering, staggering suffering, such as has never been seen before. There have been many black moments in history, but never one like this. For those who will be living in Judea (in and around Jerusalem), it will be a time to act promptly and quickly to get out of the city. It will be a time for emergency action. There will be no time left for the usual occupations of life.

These words are so fantastically suggestive that we must not hurry over them. In the words appearing in parentheses, "let the reader understand," the apostle Matthew is warning us that there are things hidden here which are not apparent on the surface. He is urging us to think, investigate, examine, and thus understand all that may be involved. We must be careful, then, to relate these words to other Scriptures, and especially to those in the Book of Daniel which Jesus specifically mentions.

Daniel's prophecy

For the present let us seek to understand this sign of the close of the age. It will be, says Jesus, "the desolating sacrilege spoken of by the prophet Daniel." No book of the Old Testament has been so unfavorably dealt with by the critics as the Book of

33

Daniel. The validity of its authorship by Daniel has been scorned and it has been ascribed to some unknown writer who lived no more than 100 to 160 years before Christ; its prophetic content has been flatly denied; and in many ways it has been more violently attacked than any other book of the Bible. Yet it is sheer presumptive arrogance for any alleged disciple of Jesus Christ to take a view of Scripture that contradicts the view of the Master. The Lord Jesus here clearly regards the Book of Daniel as a valid prophecy, inspired by the Holy Spirit, and accurate in detail.

The sign our Lord refers to is mentioned in Daniel at least three times. It is the sign of a man, a man who offers himself to the Jews to be worshipped as God. The disciples clearly understood that he was referring to the predictions in Daniel of the coming of a man who would take away the continual burnt-offering of the Jews and instead offer himself as "the abomination which makes desolate" or the desolating sacrilege. That man is described in Daniel 8:23-26:

> "And at the latter end of their rule [that is, the rule of certain kings who will come upon the world's scene in the Middle East], when the transgressors have reached their full measure [that marks the time when evil has come to its full expression], a king of bold countenance, one who understands riddles, shall arise. His power shall be great, and he shall cause fearful destruction, and shall succeed in what he does, and destroy mighty men and the people of the saints. By his cunning he shall make deceit prosper under his hand, and in his own mind he shall magnify himself. Without warning he shall destroy many; and he shall even rise up against the Prince of princes; but, by no human hand, he shall be broken. The vision of the evenings and the mornings which has been told is true; but seal up the vision, for it pertains to many days hence."

A double fulfillment

Note that Daniel was told that the vision was not concerning his own days but "pertains to many days hence." The critics insist that this was fulfilled in the turbulent days of the Maccabees in 168-165 B.C., when a Syrian king, Antiochus Epiphanes, did indeed desecrate the Temple in Jerusalem, offer a sow upon the altar, and erect a statue of Jupiter to be worshipped. But though that was undoubtedly an historic foreview of the final "abomination of desolation" it could not have been the fulfillment of Daniel's prophecy, for otherwise Jesus would not have said, more than 165 years after Antiochus, that men could yet expect to see "the desolating sacrilege spoken of by the prophet Daniel, standing in the holy place."

God's countdown

Another reference in Daniel to this sacrilege is found in chapter 9. It is in the midst of the tremendous prophecy that is called "the vision of the seventy weeks." This was an announcement to Daniel by the angel Gabriel that God had marked off a period of 490 years (seventy weeks of years), which would begin when the Persian king, Artaxerxes, issued a commandment to rebuild the walls of Jerusalem (fulfilled in 445 B.C.).* It would terminate with a period of terrible trouble during which a coming prince would cause the Jewish sacrifice and offering to cease and would thus establish the abomination which makes desolate.

The angel said that first seven, and then sixty-two of those weeks (a total of 483 years) would end just before the Messiah would be "cut off." A period of indeterminate length would then intervene before the 70th or final week (seven years). During that indeterminate period the city of Jerusalem would be

*In counting 483 years from this date, allowance must be made for a 4 year error in the date of Christ's birth (4 B.C., not A.D. 1) and the use of a 360 day year by the ancients.

destroyed and the Jews would endure wars and desolations until the end. The actual words are these in Daniel 9:26,27:

> "And after the sixty-two weeks, an anointed one [literally, Messiah] shall be cut off, and shall have nothing; [that is clearly the crucifixion] and the people of the prince who is to come shall destroy the city and the sanctuary. [This was fulfilled under Titus forty years after the crucifixion]. Its end shall come with a flood, and to the end there shall be war; desolations are decreed. And he [the prince who is to come] shall make a strong covenant with many for one week; and for half of the week he shall cause sacrifice and offering to cease; and upon the wing of abominations shall come one who makes desolate [the abomination of desolation], until the decreed end is poured out on the desolator."

The man of lawlessness

One further glimpse of this remarkable "prince who is to come" is given in Daniel 11:36-39. There he is called simply "the king."

> "And the king shall do according to his will: he shall exalt himself and magnify himself above every god, and shall speak astonishing things against the God of gods. He shall prosper till the indignation [the great Tribulation] is accomplished; for what is determined shall be done. He shall give no heed to the gods of his fathers, or to the one beloved by women; he shall not give heed to any other god, for he shall magnify himself above all. He shall honor the god of fortresses instead of these; a god whom his fathers

did not know he shall honor with gold and silver, with precious stones and costly gifts. He shall deal with the strongest fortresses by the help of a foreign god; those who acknowledge him he shall magnify with honor. He shall make them rulers over many and shall divide the land for a price."

The apostle Paul agrees

All of these passages in Daniel agree concerning the coming of a man who shall be the fulfillment of our Lord's prediction and shall be the sign of the end of the age. There are also other references in Scripture to this man. Paul is unmistakably describing the same man in II Thessalonians 2:3,4:

> "Let no one deceive you in any way; for that day will not come, unless the rebellion comes first, and the man of lawlessness is revealed, the son of perdition, who opposes and exalts himself against every so-called god or object of worship, so that he takes his seat in the temple of God, proclaiming himself to be God."

And also John

Once again, we have a clear description of him in the book of Revelation, where John describes him in 13:5-8:

> "And the beast was given a mouth uttering haughty and blasphemous words, and it was allowed to exercise authority for forty-two months; it opened its mouth to utter blasphemies against God, blaspheming his name and his dwelling, that is, those who dwell in heaven. Also it was allowed to make

war on the saints and to conquer them. And authority was given it over every tribe and people and tongue and nation, and all who dwell on earth will worship it, every one whose name has not been written before the foundation of the world in the book of life of the Lamb that was slain."

Another is coming

Before he uttered these words on the Mount of Olives, Jesus himself had referred to this coming man when he said to the rulers of the nation on one occasion, "I have come in my Father's name, and you do not receive me; if another comes in his own name, him you will receive" (John 5:43). This is that Antichrist which has been predicted in all the Scriptures, and who shall symbolize in his person all that stands against God. There are many other references to him in the Old Testament prophets but we do not have the space to consider them all.

Will the temple be rebuilt?

Perhaps you are asking, "If the Temple was destroyed by Titus in A.D. 70, what is this 'holy place' in which the Antichrist will appear?" The obvious answer is, the temple must be rebuilt in Jerusalem. The Lord is clearly indicating that there will come a time when the Jews will repossess the temple area. In view of that expectation perhaps the most important event since the first century was the capture of Old Jerusalem by the Jews in the Six Day War of 1967. For the first time in 1897 years (since A.D. 70) Jews were once again in possession of the temple site. It is now occupied by the Moslem shrine called The Dome of the Rock and the existence of that shrine raises a tremendous obstacle to the rebuilding of a Jewish temple. But there is no other place it can be built, for God decreed in the Old Testament that

Jewish sacrifices can be offered there and nowhere else on earth.

No one knows whether the present possession of Jerusalem by the Jews can be maintained. And how they will surmount the problem of rebuilding a temple on the place now occupied by an Arab holy place is anyone's guess. But rebuild it they shall, for as Jesus said in another connection, "the scripture cannot be broken." Rumors appear from time to time that plans for such rebuilding have already been completed, and even that the building itself has been partly prefabricated and is ready for assembling at almost a moment's notice. But all these reports must be taken with a grain of salt for prophetic interest is now running high and the wish is often father of the thought.

A literal event, a specific place

"When you see," said Jesus, "the man who fulfills the qualifications described in the Book of Daniel, sitting in the temple and claiming to be God, then you will know that the end of the age has arrived." It will be a literal event, to occur in a specific spot on earth at a definite moment in time. The prophecy of the seventy weeks in Daniel, already referred to, clearly indicates that there yet remains a seven year period to be inaugurated before the prophecy is fulfilled. It also declares that it is in the middle of these seven years that the Antichrist will desecrate the Jewish Temple by his claim to be God. It is evident, therefore, that it is only the last three and one half years of this seven year period which can be properly called "the end of the age." This is also designated in other places as lasting for forty-two months (Revelation 13); a time, two times, and half a time, (Daniel 7); and one thousand two hundred and sixty days, (Revelation 12). These all add up to three and one half years. Daniel also calls this "the time of the end."

But the sign of the desolating sacrilege does more than mark the beginning of this end time. It also describes it. The signs of

Scripture are never intended merely to be milestones by which we can mark off the progress of time. They are, instead, intended to reveal the hidden principles of the time in which they appear. For instance, the Jews were continually demanding of Jesus that he give them a sign that he was the Messiah. He said to them, "No sign shall be given . . . except the sign of the prophet Jonah." He went on to explain: "For as Jonah was three days and three nights in the belly of the whale, so will the Son of man be three days and three nights in the heart of the earth" (Matthew 12:39,40). His own burial and resurrection, then, was to be the sign. When that sign occurred they would understand the meaning of his coming.

The sign of the resurrection did not come at the beginning of his ministry but rather at the end. But it dramatized the meaning of his coming. It stands forever as a symbol of the new life he came to give, the new principle by which men are intended to live, a wholly new creation. The sign here is also of that nature. It is intended to mark the beginning of the end of the age, and also to indicate its character. It is a literal sign, but also symbolic.

Seeing the Invisible

If we could learn to read life rightly, almost everything is a sign. God is forever visualizing—materializing the invisible forces at work in human affairs into visible events. As we observe the events we can gain insight into what is going on behind the scenes. This is the secret behind all matter. We see visible objects around us—a table, a chair. We say we understand what it is made of—wood, plastic, or other substance. But every one who is acquainted with modern science knows that this is not the whole story. What we are seeing is the visible manifestation of invisible forces. Electromagnetic force joins together the atoms and makes up the object we see, so that what we call wood, plastic, or metal is really an invisible force making itself known in terms of a visible object. Something like this occurs in the realm of events as well as objects. When the event takes place that Jesus describes, and the Lawless One sits in the Temple of God it will be because, throughout the world, humanity has already enthroned itself as the only god man needs. The event in the Temple will be the visible representation of that world-wide fact. The day is coming, Jesus says, when the triumph of the scientific method, as we know it today, will bring man to confirm himself in the deadly delusion that he is his own god, and does not need any other. In that day the words of Psalm 2:1-3 will be fulfilled:

"Why do the nations rage, and the peoples imagine a vain thing? The kings of the earth set themselves, and the rulers take counsel together, against the LORD, and His anointed, saying, 'Let us burst their bonds asunder, and cast their cords from us.'"

But that is the day when God will laugh, says the same Psalm, and he will say, "I have set my king on Zion, my holy hill. Kiss [the Son], lest he be angry, and you perish" (vv. 6, 12). God will have the last word, though man for the moment seems to triumph.

There is a "holy place" in the human spirit. It is the place that was intended by God to be the royal residence for his Holy Spirit. Thus man can become what God intended him to be: the human expression of the divine life, the means by which the invisible God is made visible in human affairs. But in that holy place man enthrones himself instead of God, renounces all other forms of authority, and declares there is nothing greater than man.

41

The triumph of humanism

The triumph of the philosophy of humanism will not come suddenly into world affairs in the last day. The apostle Paul wrote in his own day, "the mystery of lawlessness is already at work," (II Thessalonians 2:7). It had begun even in the first century. The apostle John also wrote, already "many antichrists have" arisen (I John 2:18). No, it will not be a case of a sudden intrusion into the routine of daily human events. This idolatry of man has been building up throughout the centuries and is rapidly approaching the crisis when it will manifest itself, as the Lord describes, in a clear symbol of the times.

In our own day this lie of humanism grows gradually more powerful and persuasive. You can hear it on every side, in a thousand and one subtle variations. Recently a prominent scientist demanded that the scientific methods of observation, experiment, and logic be applied to the solution of the terrible moral and social problems of our day. Now there is nothing wrong with that idea in itself; what is wrong is the confidence expressed in his conclusion which indicated that nothing else is needed to solve men's problems. He said, "If it would [be applied] it would lead to a psychozoic kingdom [whatever that is] on earth for the ever-evolving human species." There is the empty dream, the web of illusion that man can be his own god, that he can live a full and complete life without recognition of the authority and Lordship of Jesus Christ.

You can hear this lie when someone says, "I'm not going to worry about someone else; I've got to think of myself first." It is evident in business when young men are told, "Look, if you want to get ahead in this company you've got to forget about all those old-fashioned ideas concerning cheating and lying. There really are no such things, you know. It's only thinking that makes them so." It is flung at us daily on television and radio, and every magazine paints it in living color. We are all subjected to a constant, endless din beating away at our ears, telling us that we can live complete and healthy lives without the need for God through Jesus Christ.

Glory to man

It is not that the world does not acknowledge a certain place for God, but that it is usually a very small place. It's nice to have God around once in a while, especially if you're inclined to be a bit religious. Certainly it's all right to set aside one morning a week to go to church and tip your hat to him, but you can live a perfectly wonderful life without even that. If it helps, fine, but if it doesn't, forget it. How widespread this philosophy is today! Man makes all the rules and can handle all the problems. Man exists for his own glory; down with anyone who thinks otherwise. That idea is dominant equally in the communist East and the capitalist West. Soon this widespread attitude will demand a figure, a leader, in whom all the excellencies that man sees in himself are personified. It will find its ultimate expression in a man who shall appear, to satisfy the hunger for hero worship in the world.

The end is desolation

When this man appears the world will be ready to follow him to the end. But what is that end? Listen again to the Son of God: "the desolating sacrilege spoken of by the prophet Daniel." Literally it means that abominable thing which creates desolation. How do you depict desolation? Most would think of a desert, a howling wilderness, a lifeless, dreary waste with the eternal wind moaning in torment across scorching barren sand. Already there are many lives like that today. Increasingly we hear pitiful reports of men and women, and even boys and girls, who experience nothing but futility and live lives of barren desolation. Why? Because of the abomination that makes desolate. Because of the abysmal lie that man can be his own god, that we have somehow in ourselves the adequate resources to satisfy, that we can find in some busy round of activity or pleasure that which meets the deepest need of the heart.

When men give themselves to that lie it is the abomination that makes desolate, and the desolation is in abundant evidence all around. Psychologists tell us the major problem today is meaninglessness, desolation, futility. Life is all surface and no depth. For this reason the suicide rate is rocketing to new heights. Jesus saw all this as he looked ahead across the centuries. It was little wonder, therefore, that the tears rolled down his face as he looked out over the rebellious city below him, where already the abomination which makes desolate had begun its evil work. He wept over that stubborn city as he weeps over the stubborn hearts of men today.

Rivers in the desert

Against this background of increasing desolation the gospel comes as glorious good news. When Jesus sensed the emptiness in the lives of many in his own day, he said, "If any one thirst, (Where do you thirst? In a wilderness!) let him come to me and drink . . . . 'Out of his heart shall flow rivers of living water.'" The solution for thirst in a desert is to drink, endlessly and continuously, of this fountain. There is an old hymn by Horatio Bonar that puts it very nicely.

> "I heard the voice of Jesus say,
> 'Behold, I freely give
> The living water, thirsty one.
> Stoop down, and drink, and live'
> I came to Jesus, and I drank
> Of that life-giving stream.
> My thirst was quenched, my soul revived,
> And now I live in Him."

Jesus satisfies the soul's thirst. But notice what stands in the way. It is man's pride. He does not want to stoop to drink! No one can drink of a fountain or a spring while he stands upright. He must humble himself, and stoop down, to drink. We do not like to acknowledge the fact that we are dependent, even helpless. Man resists that, and because he does he will not stoop, and if he will not stoop he cannot drink. But if he does stoop and drink, he will, as the hymn declares, *live!* It will not be but one drink but a continual drinking, and therefore, a continual living. This is God's answer to the terrible emptiness and futility of our day.

We can be sure that as the age goes on to its close, things are going to get worse. The sense of futility will deepen, the suicide rate will increase, the pressures will become more intense. Yet through all those darkening days the gospel will offer its glorious invitation, "Thirsty one! Stoop down, and drink, and live."

No one ever needs to learn to drink. Every baby is born with the ability to drink. The one thing the human heart can do without instruction is to receive. Receive Jesus Christ, drink of him, ask him to come in to be in you a fountain of living water, Master of every moment of life. In your response to that invitation, the glorious promise will begin to be fulfilled.

Prayer: Father, what amazing words were these that fell from the lips of the Lord Jesus on that day so long ago in history, so close in meaning. We ask forgiveness for the many times we have turned from his voice and heeded the lie around us. Teach us to commit ourselves alone to him, who can supply the need of our lives and meet the cry of our hearts. Let us find in him the glorious refreshment of the rivers of living water. In his name, Amen

4

When the Dam Breaks
Matthew 24:21-22

Jesus is now describing to his disciples the end of the age. That end will not be a single climactic event but a chain of events, all of which are the inevitable consequence of forces that have been at work in society throughout the whole course of this age. The Scriptures agree that the "desolating sacrilege" our Lord refers to is a man; a man of world prominence who enters the rebuilt temple in the city of Jerusalem and assumes the pre-rogatives and claims the powers of Deity. So serious is this act that it precipitates the greatest crisis the world ever will face. In Matthew 24:21,22 Jesus says of it:

> "Then there will be great tribulation, such as has not been from the beginning of the world until now, no, and never will be. And if those days had not been shortened, no human being would be saved; but for the sake of the elect those days will be shortened."

Forces at work

Many have found these words hard to believe. They clearly refer to an hour unlike anything else in history. Till recent times it had been thought incredible that humanity could ever sink to such an ebb as to bring on a judgment of this character. But we must always remember that political leaders only express ideas which have been lying half hidden in human hearts, waiting only for the precise moment to emerge. Hitler did not teach the Nazis to hate the Jews; he only dared express in voluble terms the hatred and smoldering resentment of thousands of Germans who were scarcely aware of the terrible passions hidden in their own hearts. When this man of lawlessness takes his position in the temple of God he will only be expressing what long has lain dormant in human hearts.

But though this philosophy is recognizable within us and around us, this act of man's self-deification, expressing world-wide agreement, could never occur today! You ask, "Why not?" Because there are forces at work now which restrain its full manifestation, so that it cannot take over as the dominant philosophy of the race until these restraining forces are removed. In Matthew 13:30 Jesus said, "Let both [the wheat and the tares, i.e., good and evil] grow together until the harvest." In verse 39 he said, "The harvest is the close of the age." Till that time arrives, good and evil grow together, but the dominant philosophy is not evil, but good. It is only when the harvest arrives that evil is let loose to dominate the earth.

Who's winning?

There's a little jingle that expresses the way most of us feel about right and wrong.

"Our race had an excellent beginning,
But man spoiled his chances by sinning.

47

We hope that the story,
Will end in God's glory,
But at present the other side's winning!"

It seems to many that evil is triumphant in our day. But every athletic team knows the ease by which the rival team can appear to be invincible, made up of players ten feet tall. They do everything right, while we do everything wrong. Thus it looks to many as though wrong prevails more often than right, and that we are already in the last day.

But the dominant thinking of our day, strange as it may sound to our ears, is not evil, but good! Despite widespread injustice and the terrible prevalence of violence and crime, the scales have not yet been tipped in favor of the wrong. Quite rightly do we sing, "Though the wrong seem oft so strong, God is the ruler yet."

The proof of this is that evil must constantly disguise itself as good to be able to survive. Swindlers try to appear respectable. They never boldly and blatantly label themselves crooks. Prostitutes want to be called ladies. Tyrants pose as benefactors. Liars strive to appear truthful. Cheats and misers and perverts, and a whole host of others, hunger after more respectable titles. Only good is really acceptable. Evil must dissemble and appear what it is not, to gain acceptance. This alone is ample proof that against the massive power of evil so evident today is arrayed an even more massive power for good.

Man often lives in open rebellion today, but he lives also in guilt. He knows that he needs God and in the hour of his need he often seeks God. Even communists, who in theory deny the existence of God, in practice often take great pains to disguise their evil to make it look moral and just. Occasionally they even drop expressions which indicate their own deep hunger for God. Evil is under restraint today, hemmed in by forces for good. The majority view for centuries has been truth and justice; evil is in the minority. It is powerful, but it is controlled. It is forever breaking out as cruelty and violence, in individuals, in homes and in nations, but it is ceaselessly being beaten back, overpowered and subdued again.

This accounts for the bright optimism of many who profess faith in what they call "human goodness." In their blindness they ascribe this overpowering abundance of good to man himself, and reject utterly the biblical revelation that goodness stems from the kindness of God on our behalf. In his consummate darkness man views good as an inherent trait of the human race.

Restraints removed

Jesus reveals the truth. In the end of the age, he says, it will all be different. Then evil will reign in triumphant, malicious glee. All bonds will be broken, restraints will be cast aside, and lawlessness will fill the earth. God will move in judgment, and terrible catastrophes will sweep the earth, but still men will not repent. Fear will not drive men to prayer but to further defiance. They will not wish to be delivered but only to be destroyed. They will take no delight in good, but will be made happy by the triumph of evil.

It is easy to document this by three vivid pictures from the book of Revelation. The larger part of that book traces the course of events in the Great Tribulation. It especially reveals the condition of human hearts during the time of worldwide crisis.

The first picture comes from Revelation 9:20,21:

> "The rest of mankind, who were not killed by these plagues, did not repent of the works of their hands nor give up worshiping demons and idols of gold and silver and bronze and stone and wood, which cannot either see or hear or walk; nor did they repent of their murders or their sorceries or their immorality or their thefts."

Defiance—and death

The second is from Revelation 6:12-17 and depicts the fear men experience, but the stubbornness they cherish:

> "When he opened the sixth seal, I looked, and behold, there was a great earthquake; and the sun became black as sackcloth, the full moon became like blood, and the stars of the sky fell to the earth as the fig tree sheds its winter fruit when shaken by a gale; the sky vanished like a scroll that is rolled up, and every mountain and island was removed from its place. Then the kings of the earth and the great men and the generals and the rich and the strong, and every one, slave and free, hid in the caves and among the rocks of the mountains, calling to the mountains and rocks, 'Fall on us and hide us from the face of him who is seated on the throne, and from the wrath of the Lamb; for the great day of their wrath has come, and who can stand before it?'"

The third picture, perhaps the most hideous of all, is found in Revelation 11:7-10:

> "And when they have finished their testimony, the beast that ascends from the bottomless pit will make war upon them [the two witnesses from God] and conquer them and kill them, and their dead bodies will lie in the street of the great city which is allegorically called Sodom and Egypt, where their Lord was crucified. For three days and a half men from the peoples and tribes and tongues and nations gaze at their dead bodies and refuse to let them be placed in a tomb, and those who dwell on the earth

will rejoice over them and make merry and exchange presents, because these two prophets had been a torment to those who dwell on the earth."

You can see that these are very different days from those in which we live. They may not be far removed in time, but they are far removed in character. We are drawing nearer to them all the time, but we have not yet reached the point of such blatant, unblushing and worldwide delight in evil. What will happen to bring this about? Why this terrible difference?

Restraining forces

To put the question another way: What is it that restrains the enormity of human evil today? What force is it that prevents the grinning ghouls of darkness from beginning their macabre dance of death right now? The clue is found in the Sermon on the Mount, Matthew 5. There Jesus said to the little band of disciples gathered around him—ordinary men, fishermen, tax collectors, farmers—these amazing words: "You are the salt of the earth . . . You are the light of the world" (vv. 13,14).

What did he mean? He meant they were light because they had life. John's gospel says, "In him was life, and the life was the light of men" (John 1:4). Men have light only when they are in touch with the life that comes from Jesus Christ. Here were men, simple men, who possessed life. And because they had life, they had light. They were salt, because they had savor. Jesus spoke of a salt which is without savor. It is good for nothing, he said. Men will cast it out and tread it under their feet. But here were men who had savor, a different flavor. The life they possessed, the life of Jesus Christ, made them different. It gave them a different character. It made them a different kind of people. They had a different light on their faces and a different reason for living. They had a different authority in their lives and a different power than other men.

Because of this, they were salt, arresting corruption. That is the purpose of salt. We use it in meat to stop it from spoiling, to arrest rottenness. So Jesus said they were as salt pervading society, molding human thought, challenging evil, restraining, controlling, limiting, binding, resisting the malignancy of evil in human affairs. It is for this reason that Christians must not isolate themselves from society. They must not attempt to create "Bible cities", Christian communities set off from the world, away from the stream and flow of life around them. Christians are intended to permeate every level of life. They are salt, but salt is of no value while it remains in the salt shaker!

A revealed secret

When Paul wrote to the Thessalonian Christians about the coming of the Lawless One, he said, "You know what is restraining him now so that he may be revealed in his time" (II Thessalonians 2:6). The restraining force was evidently something they knew about themselves. They had only to look into their own lives to see what restrained lawlessness within them. They knew, as we also know, that "the desires of the flesh are against the Spirit" (Galatians 5: 17). But they were also discovering that "the desires of the Spirit are against the flesh . . . to prevent you from doing what you would." The restrainer of evil is the Holy Spirit within the Christian. It is the glorious secret that Paul calls "Christ in you, the hope of glory," the life of Jesus, imparted by the Holy Spirit, acting as a dam against the manifestation of evil.

Again Paul told the Thessalonians: "He who now restrains it will do so until he is out of the way. And then the lawless one will be revealed." All restraints must be removed before what man is without God can be fully revealed. The salt must be taken out of society to allow the rottenness to be evident. When the restraints are removed man's arrogant pride will soon break out in an assumption of Deity. Then the sirens will moan, the powers of darkness will be set free, the witches of terror will ride through the sky, and the dark night of judgment will begin. "Then there will be great tribulation, such as has not been from the beginning of the world until now, no, and never will be" (Matthew 24:21).

God's timetable

When does this removal of the salt of society occur? That is the question that shrieks for an answer now. If we expect to tie it to some specific date on the calendar we are doomed to disappointment. Jesus continually warned against any attempt to set dates. But we can know the time of this removal in relation to other events at the close of the age. Since Paul says plainly that it will be before the Antichrist is revealed—"And then the lawless one will be revealed" (II Thessalonians 2:8)—we know that this removal occurs somewhere between the events recorded in verse 14 of Matthew 24, and those referred to in verse 15. It will be sometime before the desolating sacrilege spoken of by the prophet Daniel stands in the holy place.

Exactly how long before no one knows. Many Bible scholars feel it will be at least three and a half years before (at the beginning of the seven year period which is Daniel's seventieth week). This would allow some time for the corruption of society, which has been held in restraint by the presence of Christian "salt," to spread and entrench itself, and ultimately produce the worldwide delight in the blasphemies of the Lawless One when he is revealed in the temple. When all references in Scripture to this event are taken into consideration this seems to be the most likely time for the great removal to occur.

God's plan

How will it take place? By what means is the Holy Spirit taken "out of the way" so that evil is permitted to run rampant?

53

From many Scriptures the answer comes: the church is suddenly taken out of the world! This does not mean the organized, institutional church, as such. It means the true church, consisting of Christians in all denominations (and in no denomination) who possess, through the new birth, the indwelling life of Jesus Christ. As we have already seen, it is through such Christians that the Holy Spirit exercises his restraining work in society. So to remove the Christians is to remove the restraints and take the wraps off evil.

To expect such a fantastic event as this would be nothing but extreme religious fanaticism unless the Bible itself teaches that it is true. Does Jesus say anything about this? The answer is, yes! And right here in the Olivet Discourse too! He does not mention it at the time it occurs chronologically (before verse 15), but later in the message he describes it (verses 36-42), and introduces it, warning that it cannot be tied to any specific date:

> "But of that day and hour no one knows, not even the angels of heaven, nor the Son, but the Father only. As were the days of Noah, so will be the coming [*parousia*, presence] of the Son of man. For as in those days before the flood they were eating and drinking, marrying and giving in marriage, until the day when Noah entered the ark, and they did not know until the flood came and swept them all away, so will be the coming [*parousia*, presence] of the Son of man. Then two men will be in the field; one is taken and one is left. Two women will be grinding at the mill; one is taken and one is left. Watch therefore, for you do not know on what day your Lord is coming."

Two phases of His "presence"

To avoid confusion in understanding this great discourse it is important to note how clearly Jesus distinguishes between two aspects or phases of his "presence" when he returns. One is sudden, unexpected, and dateless, as we have just seen. All we know of it is that it will occur sometime before the Lawless One enters the temple and the close of the age begins. Then in verses 29,30 our Lord mentions a later phase of his presence which will occur as the final event in the close of the age:

> "Immediately after the tribulation of those days the sun will be darkened, and the moon will not give its light, and the stars will fall from heaven, and the powers of the heavens will be shaken; then will appear the sign of the Son of man in heaven, and then all the tribes of the earth will mourn, and they will see the Son of man coming on the clouds of heaven with power and great glory."

It is impossible for these "comings" to be identical. In the first, he will come without any warning or previous sign; in the second his coming will be preceded by terrible sights in the heavens, with the sun being darkened and the moon failing to give its light. In the first coming, he will appear *before* the great tribulation to remove the salt from society so evil can be loosed; in the second, he specifically says that his coming will be "immediately *after* the tribulation of those days." In the first, his coming is likened to the flood of Noah which came at a time when life was going on as usual; in the second, he will come with so much previous announcement in unusual events that "all the tribes of the earth . . . will see the Son of man coming."

When Jesus speaks about his return he is not referring to a single moment of time when he will appear, but he is talking about a return that covers a period of time. It will begin with a secret arrival, when he will come like a thief in the night. This will be the beginning of his "presence." But that presence will continue throughout all the time of trouble on earth, but behind the scenes, as it were, invisible to the world. Then, "after the tribulation of those days," he will manifest his presence visibly, appearing in power and great glory.

Here, but not here

This invisible presence of Jesus on earth is not something wholly new. During the forty days after his resurrection he was in exactly this condition. He appeared and disappeared among his disciples and they never knew when he was coming or when he would go. He was suddenly there, and just as suddenly gone. He was here, but not here. For forty days this manifestation went on until he ascended into heaven. When he comes again he will resume the same relationship to the believing Jews and Gentiles of that time. The church will be caught up to be with him, to join him in that remarkable presence during the terrible days of trouble on earth.

The church removed

The removal of the church is described also in other passages. Paul writes to the Thessalonians about that, too in I Thessalonians 4:15-18:

> "For this we declare to you by the word of the Lord, that we who are alive, who are left until the coming [*parousia*] of the Lord, shall not precede those who have fallen asleep [died]. For the Lord himself will descend from heaven with a cry of command, with the archangel's call, and with the sound of the trumpet of God. And the dead in Christ will rise first; then we who are alive, who are left, shall be caught up together with them in the clouds to meet the Lord in the air; and so we shall always be

with the Lord. Therefore comfort one another with these words."

This event is called the departure of the church. An older word for it is the "rapture" of the church. As you will note in what Paul says about it, it is intended to be a source of comfort to Christians. It is called in Titus 2:13 "our blessed hope." It means that one whole generation of Christians will not physically die, but will pass directly into a glorified state, as Jesus did on the Mount of Transfiguration before the astonished eyes of Peter, James and John (Matthew 17:2).

Don't let your imagination run away with you in trying to conceive what this event will be like. It is highly likely that it will not be visible to the world. It will be unseen and unfelt, with no disturbance of graves and nothing to indicate that anything has happened other than the strange disappearance of thousands. Just as the body of Jesus Christ was raised from the dead and passed out through the tomb without any physical manifestation whatever, so this event will take place. The stone was not rolled away from Jesus' tomb to let him out; it was rolled away to let the disciples in—so they could see what had happened. When Peter came in and found the graveclothes still lying as though wrapped around a body, but the body absent, he was convinced that something unusual had occurred.

So this will be a silent event, recognizable only by the unexplained disappearance of many. Paul describes it in I Corinthians 15:51,52:

> "Lo! I tell you a mystery. We shall not all sleep, but we shall all be changed, in a moment, in the twinkling of an eye, at the last trumpet. For the trumpet will sound, and the dead will be raised imperishable, and we shall be changed."

The whole point of our Lord's revelation of this fantastic

event is, as he puts it, "Watch therefore, for you do not know on what day your Lord is coming." Do not be deceived, do not be misled or swept off your feet by the persuasive lies of unbelief in this day. Do not be distracted by the siren sounds of a deceived society which vainly imagines that all will go on forever as it does now. Do not be deterred in your service by the growing power of evil or the dark gloom of deluded men who can switch suddenly from glowing optimism to shuddering despair. The great removal can come at any time. Are you watching?

Prayer: Thank you, Father, for the marvelous power at work in human society, arresting evil, limiting the awful rottenness of fallen human nature, so that it does not manifest itself in full power yet. Help us to be alert, aware, undeceived, available to you as you are prepared to be available to us, till the hour strikes when the restraints of grace will be removed. In Jesus' name, Amen.

5

That Strange People, the Jews

Matthew 24:16-20

Perhaps you are now thinking, "If God takes the church out of the world before the great tribulation begins, will no one have a chance to know God during that time?" To answer that perfectly proper question we must return once again to the words of Jesus to his disciples on the Mount of Olives. After he has announced the sign of the close of the age as "the desolating sacrilege spoken of by the prophet Daniel, standing in the holy place," he then adds, in verses 16-20:

> "Then let those who are in Judea flee to the mountains; let him who is on the housetop not go down to take what is in his house; and let him who is in the field not turn back to take his mantle. And alas for those who are with child and for those who give suck in those days! Pray that your flight may not be in winter or on a sabbath."

Who are they who must flee so urgently when the last days begin? Who dare not hesitate long enough even to go back into the house to pick up a wrap, but must immediately head for the hills? There is no need to wonder, for the Lord says plainly, "those who are in Judea." Now Judea is a geographical part of the land of Israel, ancient Palestine. It comprises the hill country surrounding the city of Jerusalem and includes the city as well. It is to the residents of Jerusalem and Judea that this warning is addressed.

Furthermore, the Lord's mention of the Sabbath establishes the fact that these residents of Judea are Jews. He urges them to pray that their flight will not be in the winter, with its distress of cold, or on the Sabbath, with its travel limitations, for Jews are allowed to travel only a short distance on a Sabbath day. Later in this passage these Jews are called "the elect" ("for the sake of the elect those days will be shortened"), and this makes clear that they are believing Jews, that is, men and women of faith who know and love Jesus Christ as Lord and are prepared to live or die for him.

They are not Christians in the usual sense of that term, referring to those who are members of the church, for we are told that in the church there is neither Jew nor Gentile, bond nor free. Jews are not to be distinguished from Gentiles within the church. These distinctions, we are precisely told by the apostle Paul, have been invalidated in the church. The "middle wall of partition" has been eliminated; there are no distinctions of background, race or religious training that are recognized within the church of Jesus Christ.

Furthermore, Christians, we are told, are free from the law and no longer observe special days, special feasts, new moons and Sabbaths. In his letter to the Colossians the apostle Paul clearly speaks of the fact that the Sabbaths were included in those shadows which were done away in Christ. But here the Sabbath distinctly will be a restricting factor in the flight of these people. Here then will be a class of people who cannot be identified with the present day church. They will be Jewish believers in Christ who will be converted after the removal of the church and before the time of the Great Tribulation.

A shout, a voice and a trumpet

Now a problem arises. How do these Jews become believers in Christ, since there are no Christians left to preach the gospel to them after the removal of the church? In the great description that Paul gives of the departure of the church there is a suggestive hint that may help us with this difficulty. He tells the Thessalonians that the Lord Jesus himself will descend from heaven, accompanied by three remarkable sounds. There will be, first, a shout, then the voice of the archangel, and third, the sounding of the trumpet of God. Why these three?

The shout comes from the Lord himself. As he appears to the church he will call with a loud voice. When he stood before the tomb of Lazarus he called with a great voice, "Lazarus! Come forth!" It has often been pointed out that if he had not said, "Lazarus", he would have emptied the cemetery! The great shout obviously will be to wake the dead. He had himself said, in John 5:28, "Do not marvel at this; for the hour is coming when all who are in the tombs will hear his voice [the voice of the Son of God], and come forth."

The trumpet of God is used throughout Scripture as an assembly call. A trumpet was used in the Roman army to signal the beginning of a march. In the wilderness Moses used it to summon the people of Israel to begin their journey. It is a sound directed toward the living. After the dead in Christ have been awakened by the shout of the Lord, then, Paul says, "We who are alive, who are left, shall be caught up together with them in the clouds to meet the Lord in the air." The trumpet will sound the beginning of that great gathering in of the church.

Meet Michael

Then what about the archangel's voice? Scripture refers to only one archangel. His name is Michael. He appears a number of times in the Bible and always in connection with the people of

Israel. One of the places where he is mentioned is in the twelfth chapter of Daniel, the same prophet to which Jesus referred concerning the desolating sacrilege. In verse 1 Daniel is told:

> "At that time shall arise Michael, the great prince who has charge of your people [Daniel's people, the Jews]. And there shall be a time of trouble, such as never has been since there was a nation till that time [unquestionably, the Great Tribulation]; but at that time your people shall be delivered, every one whose name shall be found written in the book."

It is strongly suggested here that Michael, the great archangel, is responsible for opening the eyes of certain Jews living in Judea at the time of the departure of the church, and that they will then recognize the Lord Jesus as their true Messiah and become believers in him.

We may link this passage with one in Revelation chapter 7:2-4, where there is a description of an event that seems to be remarkably similar, if it is not exactly the same. There the apostle John says:

> "Then I saw another angel [Here is a great angel who undertakes a special task connected with Israel. He is not called an archangel, though he well might be Michael] ascend from the rising of the sun, with the seal of the living God, and he called with a loud voice to the four angels who had been given power to harm earth and sea, saying, 'Do not harm the earth or the sea or the trees, till we have sealed the servants of our God upon their foreheads.' And I heard the number of the sealed, a hundred and forty-four thousand sealed, out of every tribe of the sons of Israel."

These 144,000 will clearly be Jews, for the passage goes on to list the twelve tribes of Israel and to declare that 12,000 are chosen from each of the tribes. Further information is given us concerning this special group in Revelation 14: 1,3-5:

> "Then I looked, and lo, on Mount Zion stood the Lamb, [Jesus] and with him a hundred and forty-four thousand who had his name and his Father's name written on their foreheads. And they sing a new song before the throne and before the four living creatures and before the elders. No one could learn that song except the hundred and forty-four thousand who had been redeemed from the earth. It is these who have not defiled themselves with women, for they are chaste; it is these who follow the Lamb wherever he goes; these have been redeemed from mankind as first fruits for God and the Lamb, and in their mouth no lie was found, for they are spotless."

The same chapter goes on to describe the Great Tribulation as "the hour of his [God's] judgment." Before that hour arrives, these 144,000 from the tribes of Israel will be seen with the Lamb on Mount Zion. This is a specific location within the city limits of Jerusalem. This account confirms the fact that Jesus Christ will be on earth during this time, and will reveal himself from time to time to these Jewish disciples, just as he appeared from time to time to his followers during those remarkable forty days following his resurrection.

Evidently these 144,000 Jews are to be turned from unbelief to belief much in the same dramatic way as was the apostle Paul. He was converted on the road to Damascus by the sudden appearance of the risen Lord Jesus Christ. Paul speaks of himself, in I Corinthians 15, as "one untimely born," very likely thinking of himself as properly belonging to this special band of Jewish believers, but who, by the grace of God, was born ahead of time and given the privilege of belonging to the church.

Israel revisited

Since these 144,000 Jews are in frequent touch with the risen Lord they will be like so many Pauls, proclaiming the eternal gospel in mighty Spirit-given power throughout the whole earth. During this time the Lawless One will be moving to consolidate his power and to present himself to the world as God. This appearance of Christ to the 144,000 is the beginning of the fulfillment of God's renewed activity with the Jews, long predicted by the Old Testament prophets. Paul also specifically says that despite the centuries of wandering following the destruction of the Temple in Jerusalem, God will not cast off his people. He will call them back again and renew a relationship with them.

In Romans 11 Paul warns that we Gentiles must never assume that God has totally and irrevocably set aside the nation of Israel, for all the promises which he has made to them in the past will be fulfilled. Because of unbelief, Paul says, God scattered them around the earth and opened the door of blessing to all the nations of earth, without distinction. But the Gentiles, too, will fail God as did the Jews, and then they will be set aside and God will call Israel back into national blessing. That is the work he will begin with the calling of the 144,000.

Will anyone believe the message these 144,000 proclaim? If they do, of course, it will probably be at the risk of their lives, since the Lawless One will soon be in full control. The answer to that question is given by the apostle John in Revelation 7:9,10,13,14:

> "After this I looked, and behold, a great multitude which no man could number, from every nation, from all tribes and peoples and tongues, standing before the throne and before the Lamb, clothed in white robes, with palm branches in their hands, and

crying out with a loud voice, 'Salvation belongs to
our God who sits upon the throne, and to the Lamb!'
Then one of the elders addressed me, saying, 'Who
are these, clothed in white robes, and whence have
they come?' I said to him, 'Sir, you know.' And he
said to me, 'These are they who have come out of
the great tribulation; they have washed their robes
and made them white in the blood of the Lamb.'"

This great multitude of Gentiles will be converted at the
eleventh hour of history, evidently by believing the gospel
preached by the 144,000 of Israel sent by the Son of God. Probably the greater part of this multitude will be martyred for their
faith. In other parts of Revelation we are told that many will be
put to death because they will not worship the Beast (the Antichrist) or his image.

Though they will indeed be "a great multitude" as John said,
yet it is immediately evident that they will be different in one
most remarkable way from the present day church. Apparently
they will not exercise the ministry of salt. They will have no soft-
ening or restraining effect upon the people around them nor on
the society in which they will live. They will be the light of the
world, of that day, exposing and thus condemning what goes on,
but they will not be salt as Christians are today, preventing corruption, restraining evil, resisting the work of injustice in society. They will live as individuals, facing, at the risk of their lives,
a society dedicated completely to a powerful delusion.

As a consequence of the fact that there will be no salt at
work in society, the dark menace of human arrogance and pride
grows darker still. Doubtless a mad science, like the Sorcerer's
Apprentice, will go blithely on, mixing evil potions and conjuring
up still more fearful forces of uncontrollable, murderous power.
It is already evident that man is convinced that he can make anything he likes. He can control the weather (he thinks); he can
build machines that can do his thinking; he can produce test-tube

babies. He has even devised a science, called biometrics, which proposes to remake man himself. The obsolete apparatus of human organization made by the Creator must be modernized. Man must be biologically rebred.

It is not only the Marxists who think man needs remaking, but also the scientists of the West who propose to turn man from a human being with an unpredictable will and an unmanageable conscience into a robot or a marionette, a compliant human vegetable. The result of these trends is completely predictable. Without realizing it, and certainly without desiring it, man in his incredible blindness has already begun to tip the delicate balance of life. Like a drunk in a canoe, he has thrown his weight around with gay abandon and, perverted by his drunken joy, he cannot see how much water has already been shipped, and that one more violent lurch is sufficient to take him to the bottom.

The apostle Peter tells us that once before in the history of the world this has happened. There was a time when man, in arrogance and pride, boasting of the civilization which he had built, quite unwittingly tripped the lever which held the world of his day in delicate balance. Before he knew what had happened, the clouds began to gather, the sky to darken, the heavens poured down floods of water, the earth heaved, the seas raised and swept across the mountaintops in monstrous waves, and all the world of man perished, except for eight souls who were safely preserved in an ark.

The fire next time

Once again, Jesus suggests, man in his clever insanity will go too far. The sign of it will be a world gone mad with self conceit, permitting and even encouraging its leaders to state publicly what almost everyone secretly believes: that there is no real God, that man is his own god and he does not need any other. Then the deadly lever will be tripped by man's own hand, the dark forces of nature will be released, the seals of nuclear power will be removed, the trumpets of human cruelty will sound out, and the vials of a demented biology will be poured out upon the earth. It is all described in detail in the book of Revelation.

Light in the darkness

About now you may be saying: "This is a terrible outlook; is there any gleam of comfort that shines through these dark clouds?" Yes, there are three things that can encourage us as we face the full implications of this remarkable word from Jesus.

First, the midnight hour has not yet arrived. Perhaps we ought to shout with gladness about that. We may be near, very near, but the hour of God's grace has not yet run its course. This is not an attempt to frighten anyone into faith, but simply a realistic facing of what Jesus Christ has said. He came into the world not to condemn it but to save. He is not interested in beating men over the head with an eschatological whip, but he does want them to see life as it is, and themselves as they are: helpless without him, in the midst of powerful forces that can sweep them to inevitable destruction.

So fantastically accurate is this long range prediction of the Lord's, and so compellingly in line with the trend of present events and attitudes, that it becomes a powerful weapon to awaken many from the dream of death in which they are engaged. There are certain questions it forces upon us: Are we spending all our waking hours living for something that is to be swept away in the rush of nuclear destruction. Or, are we living in a relationship of faith in which the Lord Jesus is living his life again in us? It is either one or the other.

The second note of encouragement is that, as always in Scripture, God's dealings with Israel are also a picture of his work with any believer. As a nation, Israel has long lived in unbelief toward the Lord Jesus Christ. They have been wandering in obscurity and persecution for many centuries. Any Christian knows that there are also times of unbelief in his own life.

67

Though he is a believer, yet he can be at times a very unbelieving believer. The result of those times of unbelief is invariably one of scattering and wandering, of darkness and distance from God.

But how beautifully this account of the 144,000 shows how God can break through such unbelief. He can bring the light of a new glimpse of Jesus streaming through the darkness just when you need it most. Perhaps you may be going through such a crisis experience where God is about to bring new light into your heart, and you will no longer walk in barrenness and darkness but in light, glory and peace. The key to such deliverance is to accept the darkness as from him, as well as the light. When we can thank him for the darkness then the light is not far away. That is what will eventually happen to Israel, and it is what God is waiting to bring about for us now.

The sovereign God—in control

The final strengthening word is that it is all happening on schedule, according to plan. It has all been anticipated and predicted. Perhaps the most comforting word the Lord Jesus ever spoke to his disciples is found in John 14:1,2: "Let not your hearts be troubled; believe in God, believe also in me. In my Father's house [the universe] are many rooms [places to live, earth is one but there are also others]; if it were not so, would I have told you that I go to prepare a place for you?" There is the comforting word. He came to set the record straight, to correct any misapprehensions. He came to outline what will happen and to set the truth before us.

It is tremendously helpful to realize that the present world events and those yet to take place are no surprise to God. Even the time of tribulation is fully known, and will not be the end of the story. Beyond the darkness lies the dawn of a new day for this weary, battered earth. Faith can lift up its eyes and strengthen its heart and rejoice that God has everything in control.

Prayer: Thank you, Lord, for the assurance you give us that you know what you are doing in history. Keep us from the stupid spirit of unbelief which treats prophetic utterances as unworthy of study and consideration. Thank you for calling us to honesty, realism, and the facing of ourselves as we really are. Help us to lay full hold of your redeeming grace and love. In Christ's name, Amen.

6

Russia, Religion and Ruin
Matthew 7:21-23; Revelation 17:1-6

Are you having difficulty in accepting some of these predicted events as true? Or do you perhaps accept them without difficulty, but yet wonder what your friends would think if you told them you believe all this? There are some who cannot tolerate detailed prediction in Scripture. They are quite content to hear prophecy as long as it deals in sweeping generalities and ambiguous figures which may be full of sound and fury, but, to them, signifies nothing. But when Scripture becomes specific and detailed, as it frequently does, they feel distressed and want to retreat to firmer ground—perhaps to the Sermon on the Mount or to some of the Lord's less explosive parables.

To talk of a Second Coming or of The Great Tribulation is, to them, almost as though you were describing an experience with little men from a flying saucer! They view the book of Revelation as a kind of eschatological Disneyland, quite unrelated to the world of space and time with which they are so familiar, or think they are. Instead of giving to prophetic Scripture the careful, thoughtful study it deserves, they throw up their hands in confusion and turn on Alfred Hitchcock or pick up a who-dunit and try to unravel that mystery instead.

Yet it seems obvious that Jesus speaks as freely about the abomination of desolation as he does of forgiveness or love. Certainly he regards the prophecies of the Old Testament in the most literal terms, adding his own predictions to them in simple, unambiguous language. He gives no hint whatever that prophecy in the future will be fulfilled in any way other than it has been fulfilled in the past, that is, simply and literally, in exact accord with what has been predicted.

Two powers—political and religious

In this chapter we will meet two forces which will be at work during the close of the age, but which are not specifically mentioned by Jesus in the Olivet Discourse. He attempts to give only a general outline of the events of that time, and we must look to other predictive Scriptures to give us the details. Jesus indicates that the Lawless One will be exercising worldwide power at the time of the Great Tribulation, but there is no specific mention of two other powers which are present during part of that time and which must be removed before the Antichrist reigns unopposed. One is a political power and the other religious.

The political power is Russia and her satellite nations. The religious rival is the false Church which is left behind when the true Church is removed. Already these forces are at work in today's world and form part of "the mystery of lawlessness" which has been continually growing since the first century. At present there is much good intermingled with the bad but when the restraints are removed the bad will quickly become much worse.

Dr. Charles Malik, formerly President of the General Assembly of the United Nations, was once asked, "What can Christians learn from the meteoric rise of world communism in

71

little more than forty years?" His answer was:

> "The most important thing to learn is that we are still living as the Germans say 'zwischen den zeiten' (between the times) when demonic forces can quickly soar very high and can take possession of the world in very short order. If it isn't Communism it will be something else: this battle between Christ and the devil is an eternal thing until Christ comes again. Christians cannot watch too closely. Christ told us to watch day and night. We don't know when he is coming again. The greatest lesson we can learn is that there is no security between the times, no security whatever."*

The Bible deals with the downfall of Russia in very short order. When you consider the amount of space that Scripture gives to what is truly important in God's sight, it is remarkable that the threat to the world and to God's cause from atheistic Russia is dealt with so briefly. The story is contained largely in two chapters from the Book of Ezekiel, chapters 38 and 39. These are supplemented by passages in Daniel 11, Joel 2 and Isaiah 10. Read these at your leisure for they help fill in the story of the fall of the great power of the north, Russia and her satellites.

Russia in prophecy

The prophet Ezekiel, in 38:1,2 identifies a great power which is coming from the north against the land of Israel. These are his words:

> "The word of the LORD came to me: 'Son of

*A Christianity Today Reader, Meredith Press, New York, 1966.

man, set your face toward Gog, of the land of Magog, the chief prince of Meshech and Tubal, and prophesy against him.'"

The land of Magog, which is mentioned also in Genesis 10, is a general term for an undefined area centering around the Caspian Sea. But the term "chief prince" is even more specific. In Hebrew it is actually "the prince of Rosh" and there is much evidence that the name Russia is derived from that word, Rosh. Scholars also identify Meshech and Tubal with the ancient capitals of Russia and Siberia, namely, Moscow and Tobolsk.

Through Ezekiel, in verses 8,9, God delivers the following message to the prince of Rosh:

> "After many days you will be mustered; in the latter years you will go against the land that is restored from war, the land where people were gathered from many nations upon the mountains of Israel, which had been a continual waste. You will advance, coming on like a storm, you will be like a cloud covering the land, you and all your hordes, and many peoples with you."

Israel invaded

It would be fascinating to trace through in detail the full revelation of Scripture concerning this coming invasion of Israel. We learn from the prophet Joel that Jerusalem will be taken and Zechariah, in his 14th chapter, gives us the details of this. Daniel adds the fact that the northern army will sweep down into Egypt and North Africa and there, having conquered these areas, the commander (Daniel calls him "the king of the north") will hear tidings out of the east and north that will trouble him and he will return into the land of Israel. There on the mountains of Judea, the very same mountains where Jesus and his disciples walked, he is to be overwhelmed and destroyed. Ezekiel 38:22,23 describes it thus:

> "With pestilence and bloodshed I will enter into judgment with him; and I will rain upon him and his hordes and the many peoples that are with him, torrential rains and hailstones, fire and brimstone. So I will show my greatness and my holiness and make myself known in the eyes of many nations. Then they will know that I am the LORD."

It is apparent from this description that God himself will assume the prerogative of dealing with the Russian threat. Whether it will involve nuclear warfare, or be purely a natural disaster, is difficult to determine. At any rate it is quite clear that the earth will never be governed from Moscow. The general consensus of biblical scholars would date this destruction of Russia some time during the first half of Daniel's seventieth week, and before the onset of the Great Tribulation.

Religious Babylon

The one roadblock to power that will remain before the Lawless One can completely have his way with the world will be the towering religious monolith which is left in control of religious affairs after the true church has been removed. The apostle John gives us a symbolic picture of this church in Revelation 17:

> "Then one of the seven angels who had the seven bowls came and said to me, 'Come, I will show you the judgment of the great harlot who is seated upon many waters, with whom the kings of the earth have committed fornication, and with the wine of whose fornication the dwellers on earth have become drunk.' And he carried me away in the Spirit

into a wilderness, and I saw a woman sitting on a scarlet beast which was full of blasphemous names, and it had seven heads and ten horns. The woman was arrayed in purple and scarlet, and bedecked with gold and jewels and pearls, holding in her hand a golden cup full of abominations and the impurities of her fornication; and on her forehead was written a name of mystery: 'Babylon the great, mother of harlots and of earth's abominations.' And I saw the woman, drunk with the blood of the saints and the blood of the martyrs of Jesus."

The ten-horned beast which this woman is seen riding is a symbolic description of the Lawless One who is the head of the political hierarchy of the western world. The woman here is the false church and she is seen riding the beast, that is, in some sense exercising control over the Lawless One.

The name of this woman is "Mystery Babylon the Great." It indicates that false Christianity is in some way linked with the ancient city of Babylon. Since Babylon is the city that grew up around the tower of Babel, as described in Genesis 11, we have in that story a strong hint of what the error of Babylonianism is. The tower of Babel was the earliest attempt of man to gain power and prestige by the exercise of religious authority. Thus there originated in the great city by the Euphrates a false religion which masqueraded as the true one and throughout all history has been infiltrating all religious systems to deceive and delude men. Its characteristics have always been the same: love of power and prestige, obtained by exercising religious authority.

Babylonianism is not confined to any one group or ecclesiastical organization today. Like the true church, the false is scattered everywhere, permeating everything. But there is this difference: the true church is an organism, a living body, made up of members who share the same life, the life of Jesus. The false church is an organization and therefore lays much stress on external membership. Wherever you find those who bow to the Lordship of Jesus Christ and love and obey him, there you have the true church. But wherever you find those who, though outwardly religious, love self and hunger after status, prestige, and the world's acclaim, there you have the false church, Babylon the Great.

It is obvious that ecclesiastical merger is the spirit of the day. Almost monthly we read of some new merger of churches or religious organizations. It appears as though the church has been infected with the Rotary Club spirit, for Rotarians love to sing, "The more we get together the happier we'll be." Despite this external merging and blending of organizations it will be impossible to separate the true church from the false until God himself will remove the true and leave the false.

Many Christians are asking, "What shall we do about this growing octopus of churches? Should we withdraw and form our own separate, purified group, where unbelief is excluded and only true Christians are admitted?" That is utterly impossible. Jesus said specifically, "Let [the wheat and the tares] grow together until the harvest." The World Council of Churches, the Roman Catholic Church, the various independent bodies, all have genuine Christians in their membership, as well as those who are Babylonians at heart. No man, or group of men, possesses the wisdom to distinguish between the true and the false. Until God makes this distinction it is necessary for each individual to judge his own heart.

Marks of counterfeit Christianity

But can you know which side you are on? Yes! The Bible indicates that there are certain attitudes which clearly mark a false Christian. Let's take a look at three incisive passages that will unveil the mark of the counterfeit. The first is from Philippians 3:18,19:

"For many, of whom I have often told you and now tell you even with tears, live as enemies of the cross of Christ. Their end is destruction, their god is the belly, and they glory in their shame, with minds set on earthly things."

One clear mark of the false is a set of wrong values. The most important thing in life to anyone is what he regards as his god. Here in this verse the god is the belly. These people are not concerned about the work of the Lord, the extension of the "good news," or meeting the needs of heartsick, hungry, or deluded people. To them the most important issues are, "What shall I eat, what shall I drink, and with what shall I be clothed." Their glory is in their shame. They glory in what really ought to be a source of shame, like a man boasting that he has bad breath. "Hallelujah, I've got halitosis!" They should be ashamed of their pride, their prejudices, and their pettiness, but instead they boast of these things and even claim they are "Christian" attitudes.

Also, they mind "earthly things." They have no vision beyond what can be seen. The earthly things are not wrong but they are not enough. The ultimate decisions of life are not to be based on immediate issues—making money, gaining or losing status, pleasing others—but on the absolute values which God declares. Jesus said, "Seek first his [God's] kingdom and his righteousness, and all these things shall be yours as well." But those who mind earthly things are always ready to forget the Lord's words when material values are at stake.

Religious workers

Another passage that marks a counterfeit Christian is Matthew 7:21-23:

"Not everyone who says to me, 'Lord, Lord,'
shall enter the kingdom of heaven, but he who does
the will of my Father who is in heaven. On that day
many will say to me, 'Lord, Lord, did we not prophesy in your name, and cast out demons in your
name, and do many mighty works in your name?'
And then will I declare to them, 'I never knew you;
depart from me, you evildoers.'"

These are people characterized by a false sense of ministry.
They are certain that what they have done will win commenda-
tion from Christ, but they are terribly mistaken. What they have
done seems quite worthy: teaching, healing and helping. "Did
we not prophesy in your name?" That is the ministry of teaching
and it is apparently Christian teaching, for it is done in the name
of Christ. "Did we not . . . cast out demons?" That is the ministry of healing, of counselling and delivering from oppressive
powers. "Did we not . . . do many mighty works?" That is the
ministry of helping. It includes such deeds as establishing
schools, building hospitals, lifting literary standards and many
other activities which the world would recognize as "mighty
works."

But there is one thing wrong. It is all accomplished for the
sake of self. It is an attempt to gain prestige and favor by doing
religious things; therefore it is Babylonianism. There has been
no new beginning, no new birth in Jesus Christ. It is perfectly
sincere, deeply earnest, even completely dedicated, but it is all
directed at the deadly magnifying of self which God completely
sets aside.

The half-hearted

One additional passage from the lips of Jesus completes the
trilogy of the counterfeit. This one is found in Revelation 3:15-
17:

"I know your works: you are neither cold nor hot. Would that you were cold or hot! So, because you are lukewarm, and neither cold nor hot, I will spew you out of my mouth. For you say, I am rich, I have prospered, and I need nothing; not knowing that you are wretched, pitiable, poor, blind, and naked."

This group suffers from a false sense of power. They think they are Christians and call themselves Christians. They even see themselves as an especially powerful church and they reckon their power from three apparent sources. The first of these is wealth. "Money talks," they say. "Money is power." But money cannot change hearts, or break evil habits, or open deluded eyes. Because they rely on money these people can never do anything more than the nearest bank or government agency can do.

Furthermore, they say, "I have prospered"; that is, increased in numbers. Is that not the standard for measuring power in many places today? "We have the largest church in town." "Our congregation is made up of the finest people and all the top leaders come." "With the votes we can sway we can do almost anything." One hears this kind of talk on every side today, but it is all a delusion of power.

As a third source of power they demonstrate a tremendous sense of confidence. "We have need of nothing," they say. "We have all that it takes to do whatever needs to be done." That is the spirit of Babylonianism. In the face of this remarkable *esprit de corps* Jesus says, "[You do not know] that you are wretched, pitiable, poor, blind and naked."

The end of the line

The ultimate fate of this false church is revealed to us by John in Revelation 17:15-17:

79

"And he said to me, 'The waters that you saw, where the harlot is seated, are the peoples and multitudes and nations and tongues. And the ten horns that you saw, they and the beast will hate the harlot; they will make her desolate and naked, and devour her flesh and burn her up with fire, for God has put it into their hearts to carry out his purpose by being of one mind and giving over their royal power to the beast, until the words of God shall be fulfilled.'"

Shorn of its real power by the removal of the true Christians, the whole ecclesiastical structure becomes nothing but a hollow mockery. Though it still attempts to ride the beast, and thus to continue the moral control and political influence it has always exercised, yet this soon becomes no longer possible. Morality without faith is empty and vain and it cannot long survive for it has no power. When the hypocrisy of this false church becomes no longer concealable the nations will turn on it like wild pigs and rend the whole hypocritical structure to the ground.

There was an historical foreview of this in the days of the French Revolution. Then, during the revolt against established religion, cathedrals were torn down or turned into marketplaces, altars were violated, prostitutes were invested as priests, and religious teachings were held up to scorn. So also the nations will hate the harlot and make her desolate and naked, devouring her flesh and burning her with fire. Then the Lawless One will be free to carry out his cruel will upon the peoples of earth.

If in searching your own heart you find a continual manifestation of self-centeredness, of concern for yourself and lack of concern for others, of bitterness or resentment, all these mark the path of unbelief. Though you may have received the Lord Jesus into your heart, you are not yet living the life he came to give you. Ask him to deal with the pride and love of position within you and to make your heart flame with his life, love, grace, glory and joy. If life is dull and meaningless to you, uncertain and filled with darkness, then somewhere you've failed to take what he came to give.

He did not come to give you darkness, dullness, and drabness. He came to give life—abundant life; the kind that he himself lived in the days of his flesh. If he has entered your heart then expect him to live that kind of life in you, for that is what the Christian life is: all of him being all that he is, in you! Nothing less than this is true Christianity.

Prayer: Thank you, Heavenly Surgeon, for the sharp knife of your Word which pierces into the inner parts of our lives and cuts away the cancerous growths of pride and self-sufficiency. Thank you also for the life of the Lord Jesus which is given to us by faith. Teach us how to live in continual expectation of his activity in us, that we may be real, and not counterfeit, Christians. In his name, Amen.

7

The Secret Presence
Matthew 24:23-28

Do you know the first question ever asked in the New Testament? It was asked by Wise Men who came out of the East to Jerusalem, saying, "Where is he who has been born king of the Jews?" A little later Herod the king asked the same question of the scribes, "Where (is the Christ) to be born?" They told him, "In Bethlehem of Judea." Thus the New Testament opens with a search for Christ, "Where is he?"

As Jesus stands on the Mount of Olives with his disciples and previews for them the remarkable period to come which he calls, "the close of the age," he indicates that during that time men will still be asking, "Where is the Christ?" But then, he says, it will be a trick question; be careful of it! In Matthew 24:23-28, he says:

> "Then if any one says to you, 'Lo, here is the Christ!' or 'There he is!' do not believe it. For false Christs and false prophets will arise and show great signs and wonders, so as to lead astray, if possible, even the elect. Lo, I have told you beforehand. So, if

they say to you, 'Lo, he is in the wilderness,' do not go out; if they say, 'Lo, he is in the inner rooms,' do not believe it. For as the lightning comes from the east and shines as far as the west, so will be the coming of the Son of man. Wherever the body is, there the eagles will be gathered together."

Do not miss the time word with which Jesus opens this section. *"Then* if any one says to you," etc. "Then" clearly refers to the time of the Great Tribulation which he has briefly but terribly described with the words, "if those days had not been shortened, no human being would be saved." As we have seen, this is the last three and one-half years of Daniel's predicted seventieth week. During this terrible time of persecution and judgment the Lord Jesus will support and sustain his own by appearing to them frequently in a variety of places. These appearances will certainly be made to the 144,000 in their worldwide ministry, and perhaps also to that "great multitude" of Gentile believers who will come out of the Great Tribulation.

As a result of this rather unusual state of affairs, rumors will apparently spread like wildfire that Jesus Christ is somewhere around.

In John 7:11,32-36 Jesus himself predicted that a situation like this would occur during the forty day period after his resurrection:

"The Jews were looking for him at the feast, and saying, 'Where is he?' [There's that question again! A little further on John says:] The Pharisees heard the crowd thus muttering about him, and the chief priests and Pharisees sent officers to arrest him. Jesus then said, 'I shall be with you a little longer, and then I go to him who sent me; you will seek me and you will not find me; where I am you cannot

83

come.' The Jews said to one another, 'Where does this man intend to go that we shall not find him? Does he intend to go to the Dispersion among the Greeks and teach the Greeks? What does he mean by saying, "You will seek me and you will not find me," and, "Where I am you cannot come"?'"

To these Jews Jesus was nothing but a tub-thumping, rabble-rousing, troublemaker from Nazareth and they intended to put him to death as quickly as possible. Jesus knew this and knew that they would succeed in their plans. But now he puzzled them completely by telling them that after they had done their worst, they would look for him but would not be able to find him. That could have been true only during his forty-day post-resurrection ministry. After he ascended into the heavens they did not look for him, for the disciples were then declaring throughout Jerusalem that he had gone to the Father. But during that forty-day period there must have been many disquieting rumors, which came to the authorities' ears, that Christ was still somewhere around.

When the soldiers came from the grave of Jesus with the report that he had risen from the dead, they had to be bribed to say that his disciples had come and stolen his body away, and thus to quiet that rumor. But soon other rumors were buzzing. Mysterious appearings of Jesus to his disciples were reported and the authorities must have sent out many search parties to try to locate him. But as Jesus had predicted, they searched for him but they could not find him. They could never understand the reason, but it was exactly as he had said: "Where I am you cannot come." In the new relationship to his own into which he had entered, it was impossible for them to intrude.

Pre-church and post-church Christians

During that forty-day period the disciples of Jesus were what we might call "Pre-church Christians." They believed in Jesus but they were not yet members of the church, for the church was not formed until the day of Pentecost when the Holy Spirit was poured out. During the close of the age, the disciples (or as Jesus calls them, "the elect") will be what we might call "Post-church Christians." The church has been removed from the world, at least from any visible participation in world affairs. Since we know that Christians will be given glorified bodies like their Lord's (and Paul says that, once removed from this life, the church will be forever "with the Lord"), it seems highly likely that church Christians will join the Lord Jesus in this ministry behind the scenes during the tribulation. They will be like Moses and Elijah who appeared with the transfigured Christ on the Mount.

The picture then is clear. Jesus will come for his church and take the members into a new relationship with him. Then he, with them, will remain throughout the "end of the age" period, appearing only to those whose hearts are ready to believe in him. Rumors of his presence will continually be spread abroad, so that men will be saying in that day as they said during the forty-day period, "Where is he?" Authorities will search for him and will not be able to find him, but false prophets will claim to know where he is.

Masters of deceit

Part of the tribulation of the end times will be a fresh and powerful campaign of deceit which will break out against any who are tempted to believe in Jesus. Just as the Lord foresaw and described the great forces of deceit which would be at work until the close of the age arrived, so he also describes those which will be dominant during the Great Tribulation.

Their first element will be the presence of authoritative personalities. "False Christs and false prophets will arise" (Matthew 24:24). No program of falsehood among men ever existed without a masterful or powerful leader. The human heart inveterately loves a good showman. Men tend easily to follow those who speak with authority and who manifest drive and dash in their personalities. And there is no road to error quite so compelling as a religious one. History confirms the idea that more people are misled religiously than any other way. Let a blatant atheist utter an attack against Christianity and no one is greatly disturbed or changed. But let a bishop of the church, dressed in religious garb and using pious language say the same thing and immediately it is discussed and openly or secretly admired all over the world.

So false Christs shall arise, taking full advantage of the superstitious expectancy of the times, for, as Jesus said in another place, "Men [will be] fainting with fear and with foreboding of what is coming in the world." They will come with a display of signs and wonders, misleading many, and playing ultimately into the hand of the Lawless One.

Not only will there be false Christs, but also false prophets. We have already seen that this can have a secular sense: the pacesetters of thought, philosophers, professors, scientists; clever men of great intelligence who are listened to when they talk. While the church is yet on earth it acts as salt, pervading every section of life, and there are men of true faith found among the prophets of the world everywhere today. But in that day there will no longer be room for the gospel of the supernatural; there will be no place among intellectuals for what Paul calls a "secret and hidden wisdom of God," which none of the princes of this world knew, for had they known it, they would never "have crucified the Lord of glory" (I Corinthians 2:7,8).

Since there will no longer be a place among the leaders of the world for those who live by faith, there will arise men of tremendous intellectual capacity and ability who will become the instruments of error—false prophets—who will convince millions that the lie of Antichrist is the only reasonable basis for life.

The lure of the lie

Augmenting the pull of masterful personalities in the last days, will be also the power of persuasive propaganda. As we have already noted, powerful rumors of the mysterious presence of Jesus Christ will sweep the nations. There will be many who will claim to have authoritative information as to where he may be found. They will offer themselves as privileged companions of Christ, claiming that they alone may be trusted to lead the seeker to him.

Lest this seem almost unbelievable, let me share a personal experience which occurred a few years ago. I was invited to meet a certain Bible teacher in a private home. He told me, without much preamble "Christ has already returned to earth and I happen to belong to a group of people who know where he is. If you are really interested in preaching the truth, I can tell you how to get in on the inner secrets."

I was not deeply impressed, and said to him, "Where is he, then, since you claim to know?"

"Oh, he is in a special place in the desert, here in California," he answered. "I have seen him many times and others that I know have seen him. Only we know where he is."

To learn what he would say, I turned to this very passage of Scripture and read these words to him: "If [a man says] to you, 'Lo, he is in the wilderness,' do not . . . believe [him]."

"Oh," he said, "Jesus didn't mean our group!"

Well, that is the crack-pot approach to prophecy. But the false Christs and their followers in the last days will say the same thing. They will relate their offer to various longings of the heart. To some who have grown tired of the rat race of life and are especially fed up with city living, they will say: "Lo, he is in the wilderness." They will suggest that the nature of the Messiah's message is a call to return to nature, to simplify life and get back to the primitive struggle of wrestling with the elements.

Others will make appeal to the lust for knowledge. They will

87

say that the Christ can only be found in the race to unlock the mysteries of the universe. The answer will be found in the inner rooms of knowledge. When we know what we are and who we are and how we operate, then we will be able to find the mysterious presence of the Messiah. He is in the inner rooms, if anywhere at all.

Does this sound familiar? In the end of the age it will not be necessary to invent any new ideas. It will only be necessary to augment the ones that are already current in life.

As a final clincher, Jesus says that these false leaders will "show great signs and wonders, so as to lead astray, if possible, even the elect." Even this is nothing new. The man on the street today is so impressed by the wonders science has brought about that he is ready to believe anything is possible.

When the first H-bomb was exploded in the Pacific one reporter described the blast as, "White and hot, like the flash of a breaking electrical circuit. It turned almost instantly to bright bilious green, a color so unexpected that watchers on the beach gasped. Great green fingers of light poked out through the clouds. From the center of the blast a red glow began expanding upward. It was not the familiar orange of the tropical sunset, but a deep solid red, and the people afterwards groped for words to describe it. The glow bubbled aloft and boiled into the sky. A quarter moon—some people thought it was the fire-ball— showed through occasionally as the clouds broke and its face glowed, not pale, but a rich, strange yellow."

Another reporter on the island of Samoa reported seeing a rainbow with colored lights dancing. "Later," he said, "the rainbow faded, but it left something behind that I had never felt with rainbows—elation, awe, and an unearthly fright." When man can conjure up spirits as frightful as that, who is not ready to listen? What a witches' brew of wonders will be released when "the mystery of lawlessness" in its final form makes a last, final, desperate effort to capture men's minds and sweep them over the precipice of deceit to destruction.

The false—now, the true

In contrast to the false propaganda of the last days, in Matthew 24:27,28 Jesus unveils the true method for locating him in the day of his presence. To do so he uses a parable from nature and a proverb from life:

> "For as the lightning comes from the east and shines as far as the west, so will be the coming of the Son of man. Wherever the body is, there the eagles will be gathered together."

The word the Lord uses for "coming" here is the now familiar "parousia." It is quite a different word than he uses a few verses farther on when he speaks of "the Son of man coming on the clouds of heaven with power and great glory." It is easy to confuse these two comings because of his reference to lightning in verse 27. Since lightning is a form of power and glory many feel the Lord is using it as a symbol of his coming in glory. But note carefully what he says.

Lightning flashes in the east, but the effect of it is seen over all the sky. Yet the flash itself does not involve the whole inverted dome of the heavens from east to west. When he uses the symbol of lightning, therefore, he is not describing a universally visible manifestation of his glory, but the universal effect of his presence behind the scenes. Like lightning flashes he will be seen by his own in different places, at different times, but the effect of those appearances will be felt throughout the earth.

Furthermore, lightning is sovereign, unpredictable, uncontrollable. So will be the presence, the *parousia,* of the Son of man. He will appear and disappear at will. Whenever there is need for him he will be there, just as he was during the post-resurrection period. There will be no need to search for him for he cannot be found that way. There will be no need to look for him in the wilderness nor in the inner rooms, for he will come whenever and wherever he finds a heart ready to know him. In the passage parallel to this in Luke 17, Jesus says, "For as the lightning flashes and lights up the sky from one side to the other, so will the Son of man be *in his day*." A "day" used in that sense always refers to a period of time, not a sudden, climactic event.

Then, using a common proverb of the day, Jesus indicates the proper way to find him in that day, "Wherever the body is, there the eagles will be gathered together." Rather than eagles, the margin gives the proper word, vultures: "there the [vultures] will be gathered together."

When I was a boy in a remote high school in Montana, we were having basketball practice one night. At the close of the practice period the coach called one of the team members aside. I watched him go to the other side of the room. The boy was a close friend of mine and came from a rather poor family who were trying to eke out a living on a ranch about ten miles north of town. As I watched the lad's face while the coach was talking to him, I saw it blanch and after a bit the boy walked off with his head down. The coach came over to us and said, "I just gave Joe some bad news. His dad has been found dead." Then he told us how he was found.

One of the neighbors owned a ranch about four or five miles away, but separated from Joe's home by a deep canyon. This man had looked over and noticed that there was no smoke rising from the ranch house, so he saddled a horse and rode over. When he came to the silent cabin and found no one around he began to wonder if anything had happened. As he looked about he saw in the sky, about a half mile off, a number of birds circling. As he watched he saw they were buzzards, a type of vulture. Mounting his horse again he rode off to investigate. Beneath the spot where the buzzards circled he found the body of Joe's father. I have never forgotten that incident, and every time I read this verse I think of it. "Wherever the body is, there the [vultures] will be gathered together."

Unmistakable marks

What does the Lord mean by this? Does he mean that he is like a body, a decaying corpse? Would this be what we might term a dead giveaway? No, he is simply taking a common parable which meant that whenever the question of "where" arises about a subject, then look for some identifying activity. We have a similar proverb today, "Where there's smoke, there's fire."

In that day men will ask, "Where is Jesus Christ? How do you find him? Where is he?" The answer is, wherever you see the signs of his activity. They are always unmistakable. He comes to transform life, to make it over anew. He comes to remove delusion and deceit and to lead instead into truth and reality. He comes to deliver from guilt, from fear, and from hate. Even in those terrible days of unheard-of violence, cruelty, and death, he will be busy with his everlasting ministry. If you want to know where he is working, look for the sign of transformed lives.

It has always been true. It will be true in the days of his glorified presence on earth, but it is also true now, in the day of his spiritual presence. He is sovereign, uncontrollable, unlimited by geography. False faiths forever say, "We have a corner on Christ," but the true faith says he is universally available. He is at the instant disposal of any heart which in humility and contriteness is ready to do business with him.

Prayer: Heavenly Father, it is wonderful to know that we find Jesus Christ, not by searching up and down the earth, nor by delving into esoteric realms of knowledge, nor by probing into secret and mysterious teachings from the past, but by a simple, honest facing of our own need and a response to his invitation to us. Save us from the awful blasphemy of pretending to be Christians without having known a transformed life. Keep us from the false front, the facade. In Jesus' name, Amen.

8

The Power and the Glory
Matthew 24:29-31

The most dramatic event in all history will be the visible appearing of Jesus Christ. No one can possibly miss it when it occurs. He himself describes it for us in Matthew 24:29-31:

> "Immediately after the tribulation of those days the sun will be darkened, and the moon will not give its light, and the stars will fall from heaven, and the powers of the heavens will be shaken; then will appear the sign of the Son of man in heaven, and then all the tribes of the earth will mourn, and they will see the Son of man coming on the clouds of heaven with power and great glory; and he will send out his angels with a loud trumpet call, and they will gather his elect from the four winds, from one end of heaven to the other."

This is the most prophesied event in the Bible. The Old Testament contains many references to it, and it has been estimated that in the New Testament one verse out of ten refers to this coming of Jesus Christ. If all the references to this event were taken out of the New Testament, you would find it unintelligible in many parts.

From "presence" to unveiling

But we must be careful to understand this visible appearing of Jesus in relation to the *parousia,* the presence of Jesus, which will begin after the Church is taken out of the restrictions of time before the end of the age begins. This flaming advent is also part of the *parousia* and is actually the event that marks the end of the secret presence. It is the outshining of his presence before the eyes of the whole world. What he has been in secret to his own during the dark days of the tribulation, he now will be openly before the whole world. Especially will he manifest himself to the Lawless One. Paul says, "The Lord Jesus will slay him with the breath of his mouth and destroy him by his appearing and his coming" (II Thessalonians 2:8).

That last phrase, "his appearing and his coming," is literally, "the epiphany of his *parousia.*" Epiphany is a word that means unveiling, or outshining. Taken in that sense, Paul is calling this dramatic appearance of Jesus Christ, "the unveiling of his presence." It is the startling climax of the whole period which Jesus calls, "the close of the age."

Civilization's last hour

The final crashing crescendo of civilization's last hour will be accomplished in three sweeping movements. Each of these is traced in broad strokes by Jesus. The first is a violent activity in nature:

> "Immediately after the tribulation of those days the sun will be darkened, and the moon will not give its light, and the stars will fall from heaven, and the powers of the heavens will be shaken."

93

Notice that the Lord Jesus distinctly separates this event from the Great Tribulation. The tribulation will be essentially the manifestation of the naked brutality of man, the exhibition of the cruelty and unbelievable violence of the human heart unrestrained by grace. It is described for us in detail in the book of Revelation, especially in the judgments of the seals and the trumpets. It will be a time when the horrors of Nazi persecution, reflected in the gas chambers of Buchenwald and Dachau, will be repeated all over the earth; a time when violence stalks the streets, and the nuclear witches of terror scream through the skies. As Jesus said, it will be a day of unprecedented human evil, of terrible slaughter and human suffering.

But immediately following this tribulation terrifying signs appear in the heavens. The phrase, "the powers of the heavens will be shaken," suggests severe gravitational disturbance of the solar system. This in turn would produce phenomenal effects on the earth. Showers of meteors will flash through the darkening skies. Earthquakes cause the land to heave and shake, and great tidal waves sweep the coasts. Luke reports that, "men [will be] fainting with fear," and that there will be great "distress of nations in perplexity at the roaring of the sea and the waves." Volcanos erupt, spouting out streams of lava and vast clouds of cinder and ash which obscure the sun and moon. The sun is darkened and the moon reddens and is finally unable to shine at all.

Unbelievable as all this may sound to our ears, nevertheless it very likely does not include anything which has not happened before within the memory of mankind! The Russian scientist, Immanuel Velikovsky,* has amassed a tremendous amount of evidence from many sources indicating, quite apart from any religious connotation, that in the past there have occurred similar times of volcanic eruption, seismic activity, and disturbances in the solar system. It is the conviction of this scientist that the

*Worlds in Collision, Doubleday & Co., Garden City, New York, 1950.

plagues of Egypt during the time of the Exodus under Moses were part of a world wide upheaval in nature caused by a comet closely approaching this earth. Its gravity drew the waters of the sea into huge tidal waves and caused volcanos to disgorge great flows of lava which came pouring from the mountain ranges of earth. The comet then went on to become the planet Venus, which often appears in our sky as the morning star.

These theories are disparaged in some scientific circles, but all agree that Velikovsky has gathered together an enormous amount of evidence for strange happenings in the past. The discoveries of the rocket "Voyager" on its trip to Venus helped to confirm certain claims of Velikovsky concerning the nature of this planet and its origin, and there is now much scientific interest in Venus.

Even in relatively modern times there are many unexplained celestial phenomena. By no means should we assume that science is able to explain all that has taken place in even the immediate past. In one of his public speeches while president, John F. Kennedy mentioned the unexplained Dark Day which occurred in the month of May, 1780, when all of New England was for many hours plunged into total darkness. No one has ever been able to explain it, but it remains a fact of history. From time to time the papers report the falling to earth in various places of great chunks of ice weighing sometimes four to five hundred pounds. No one yet knows their origin.

Voices from the past

To face honestly the unresolved mysteries of the past is to realize afresh how readily these words of Jesus can be fulfilled. It is not only Jesus who tells us of these earth traumas, but other prophets from the Old Testament have foretold them. For instance, Joel 2:30,31 says:

"And I will give portents in the heavens and on

95

the earth, blood and fire and columns of smoke. The sun shall be turned to darkness, and the moon to blood, before the great and terrible day of the LORD comes."

Isaiah also describes the same event, using very similar language in 13:9,10:

"Behold, the day of the LORD comes, cruel, with wrath and fierce anger, to make the earth a desolation and to destroy its sinners from it. For the stars of the heavens and their constellations will not give their light; the sun will be dark at its rising and the moon will not shed its light."

And in Revelation 6:12-14, the apostle John describes it in very vivid terms.

"When he opened the sixth seal, I looked, and behold, there was a great earthquake; and the sun became black as sackcloth, the full moon became like blood, and the stars of the sky fell to the earth as the fig tree sheds its winter fruit when shaken by a gale; the sky vanished like a scroll that is rolled up, and every mountain and island was removed from its place."

All these passages confirm the words of Jesus that some celestial force will create these tremendous events upon earth, and will thus introduce the final act in the drama of civilization as we know it.

The unveiling of Christ

This violent upheaval in nature is followed immediately by

the sign of the Son of man in heaven and the visible appearing of Jesus Christ to all the earth:

> "Then will appear the sign of the Son of man in heaven, and then all the tribes of the earth will mourn, and they will see the Son of man coming on the clouds of heaven with power and great glory."

As we have already noted, this is the outshining of his glory; the sudden unveiling of his presence. It is often called "the second coming," though in truth that term covers the whole period of Christ's secret presence. But it will be the second time the world sees Jesus Christ. The last time it saw him was on a bloody cross, writhing in the agonies of death, apparently a shameful failure with no glory, no power and no success. But when it sees him again it will see him coming triumphant in power and glory.

The event will be preceded by the appearance of "the sign of the Son of man" in the heavens. The disciples had asked him at the beginning of this discourse: "What will be the sign of your coming?" This question he now answers, though not as completely or clearly as they or we might have liked.

When the disciples asked the question they did not mean, as we frequently take it, "What is the sign that will mark the time of your coming?" Inevitably we associate signs with schedules. But the disciples knew better than that. They meant, "What is the event which will reveal the meaning of your coming?" This is always the purpose of signs in Scripture. That sign, Jesus now says, will appear in the sky just before he is made visible.

Let us not miss the fact that he links this sign with the statement, "then all the tribes of earth will mourn." We shall examine that more fully a bit later, but from other Scripture it appears that he means the tribes of Israel. Since this sign is thus linked with Israel it strongly suggests that the sign will consist of the reappearance of the cloud of glory which accompanied the nation

Israel as they journeyed through the wilderness for forty years. It was called the Shekinah, and was the sign of God's presence with his people. Much later, when the Temple was built and Solomon dedicated it to God, the Shekinah glory came down and took rest in the holy of holies upon the Ark of the Covenant as the sign that God was dwelling with his people.

God with us—in power

This shining cloud may well be what Jesus himself is referring to when he says, "They will see the Son of man coming *on the clouds* of heaven." There is an obvious reference to this same event in Revelation 1:7. There John says:

> "Behold, he is coming with the clouds, and every
> eye will see him, every one who pierced him; and all
> tribes of the earth will wail on account of him."

Of course it can simply refer to the atmospheric clouds, but the repeated emphasis seems suggestive of more. When Jesus thus appears it will mark the close of the age, but it will also be the opening event of a new age and the supreme characteristic of that new age will be that God dwells with his people. In Revelation 21:3, John describes it, "Behold, the dwelling of God is with men. He will dwell with them, and they shall be his people, and God himself will be with them." Since the Shekinah is the sign of God's presence with man, it is fitting that it should reappear as the sign that explains, clarifies, and reveals the meaning of Christ's coming. He comes that he may be, as the Old Testament prophets whispered, "Immanuel—God with us!"

The shining cloud will be followed by the dramatic appearance of Jesus Christ himself. It is not a silent appearing, not something that takes place in a corner, but a bold, triumphant revelation. As we have seen, John declares that every eye shall see him. In II Thessalonians 1:7,8, Paul speaks of a time:

"When the Lord Jesus is revealed from heaven with his mighty angels in flaming fire, inflicting vengeance upon those who do not know God and upon those who do not obey the gospel of our Lord Jesus."

The present age, when God allows man to have his head, is brought to an end and God now reasserts his right to rule over all the earth. It is described in striking language in Revelation 11:15:

"Then the seventh angel blew his trumpet, and there were loud voices in heaven, saying, 'The kingdom of the world has become the kingdom of our Lord and of his Christ, and he shall reign for ever and ever.'"

The reference of Jesus to his coming "with power and great glory" reminds us immediately of the closing words of the Lord's Prayer. How many times have you prayed, "For thine is the kingdom, the power, and the glory"? That prayer reflects the anticipation of God's people, through all the dark centuries, of the eventual coming of that flaming hope when the power and the glory of the universe will be in the hands of the One to whom it rightfully belongs.

It was to prevent this that the tempter met Jesus in the wilderness at the beginning of his ministry and tempted him three times. The final temptation was to take him to a high mountain and show him all the kingdoms of the world in a moment of time. There the devil said, "All these I will give you, if you will fall down and worship me." In effect he was saying, "Mine is the kingdom, the power, and the glory." And he was right!—for the moment. Jesus did not rebuke him for some preposterous claim that had no justification. Rather he answered him, using the only weapon that is available to a believer in any hour of darkness or temptation, the unchangeable word of God. He said to him: "It is written, 'You shall worship the Lord your God and him only shall you serve.'"

With those words Jesus set aside the temptation to take a seeming short-cut to the goal for which he came. Instead he went on to the darkness of the cross, the agony and blood of death, in order that he might make possible the hour he is describing here, when he will come to take the kingdoms of the world, in power and great glory.

When Israel mourns

The unveiling of Jesus as Lord of lords and King of kings will also accomplish certain immediate events. The first will be the mourning of the nation Israel. As we have already noted, the Lord's reference to "all the tribes of the earth will mourn" does not mean tribes of Indians, but tribes of Jews. In the verse from Revelation already quoted, John says, "All tribes of the earth will wail on account of him." It will be the mourning of Israel in her hour of national sorrow.

Their mourning will be in direct fulfillment of the prophecy of Zechariah 12:10,11:

> "And I will pour out on the house of David and the inhabitants of Jerusalem a spirit of compassion and supplication, so that, when they look on him whom they have pierced, they shall mourn for him, as one mourns for an only child, and weep bitterly over him, as one weeps over a first-born. On that day the mourning in Jerusalem will be as great as the mourning for Hadadrimmon in the plain of Megiddo."

Why will they mourn? Because they will be looking on him whom they have pierced. To their utter astonishment they will discover that the One who appears in power and great glory bears in his hands the marks of nails and in his side the wound of a spear. Of course, all the world is guilty of piercing the Son of God, but the Jews were particular instruments in that respect.

Perhaps the very words of their mourning are recorded for us in a well-known passage from the prophet Isaiah. In the day that Israel shall look on him whom they have pierced, they will say to each other:

> "Who has believed what we have heard? And to whom has the arm of the LORD been revealed? For he grew up before him like a young plant, and like a root out of dry ground; he had no form or comeliness that we should look at him, and no beauty that we should desire him. He was despised and rejected by men; a man of sorrows, and acquainted with grief; and as one from whom men hide their faces he was despised, and we esteemed him not. Surely he has borne our grief and carried our sorrows; yet we esteemed him stricken, smitten by God, and afflicted. But he was wounded for our transgressions, he was bruised for our iniquities; upon him was the chastisement that made us whole, and with his stripes we are healed."

They will recognize in that day that the one whom their fathers, in ignorance and blindness, had crucified was the one who had loved them and given himself for their sins. They will cry out in sadness and heartache over the long years of rejection that have followed his crucifixion.

Righteousness triumphs—at last!

But that is not all that will happen to Israel when Jesus appears in power and glory. He also adds, concerning himself,

"He will send out his angels with a loud trumpet call, and they will gather his elect from the four winds, from one end of heaven to the other."

Once again we do not need to be in doubt as to who these elect are. Isaiah 11:11,12 helps us here:

> "In that day [the context makes clear it is the end of the age] the Lord will extend his hand yet a second time to recover the remnant which is left of his people, from Assyria, from Egypt, from Pathros, from Ethiopia, from Elam, from Shinar, from Hamath, and from the coastlands of the sea.
> "He will raise an ensign for the nations, and will assemble the outcasts of Israel, and gather the dispersed of Judah from the four corners of the earth."

Jeremiah also confirms the same promise. The whole thirty-first chapter of Jeremiah should be read to note the beauty of its language and the lilting gladness of its promise. But in verses 7,8, he says:

> "' . . . the LORD has saved his people, the remnant of Israel.' Behold, I will bring them from the north country, and gather them from the farthest parts of the earth, among them the blind and the lame, the woman with child and her who is in travail, together; a great company, they shall return here."

Certainly this gathering will include the 144,000. Perhaps also it will include as many as are left alive of the "great multitude" of Gentiles who believe in Jesus because of the testimony of the remnant of Israel. Jesus himself, in his description of this same gathering given in the parables of Matthew 13, suggests that others are included. He says, in verses 40-43:

> "Just as the weeds [tares] are gathered and
> burned with fire, so will it be at the close of the age.
> The Son of man will send his angels, and they will
> gather out of his kingdom all causes of sin and all
> evildoers, and throw them into the furnace of fire;
> there men will weep and gnash their teeth. Then the
> righteous will shine like the sun in the kingdom of
> their Father."

Many have confused this gathering by the angels with the
removal of the church, described by Paul in I Thessalonians 4.
Nothing is said here of gathering the elect into heaven, but
rather, as ordinary living persons, they are gathered into an
earthly kingdom. There is no resurrection of the dead mentioned at all, while in the case of the removal of the church, this
is a primary emphasis.

Furthermore, when the church is removed there is no sug-
gestion that evil men are judged, but in the passage quoted
above from Matthew 13, Jesus makes clear that "all causes of
sin and all evildoers" will be removed from his kingdom at the
same time that the elect are gathered. This he emphasizes further in another of the Matthew 13 parables, verses 47-50:

> "Again, the kingdom of heaven is like a net which
> was thrown into the sea and gathered fish of every
> kind; when it was full, men drew it ashore and sat
> down and sorted the good into vessels but threw
> away the bad. So it will be at the close of the age.
> The angels will come out and separate the evil from
> the righteous, and throw them into the furnace of
> fire; there men will weep and gnash their teeth."

Doubtless it will be at this time that the Lawless One will
come to his end as it is described by John in Revelation 19:19-
21:

"And I saw the beast and the kings of the earth with their armies gathered to make war against him who sits upon the horse [the Lord Jesus] and against his army. And the beast was captured, and with it the false prophet who in its presence had worked the signs by which he deceived those who had received the mark of the beast and those who worshiped its image. These two were thrown alive into the lake of fire that burns with brimstone. And the rest were slain by the sword of him who sits upon the horse, the sword that issues from his mouth; and all the birds were gorged with their flesh."

The Jew and you

In this review of his dramatic return to earth, the Lord Jesus has laid great stress upon its effect upon Israel. Probably you, like the vast majority today, are not Jewish but Gentile. You may well ask, "What significance has all this for me?" As we have already noted, whenever God wants us to understand how he will handle us as believers today, he holds before us the history of the nation Israel.

Briefly retrace the history of this race and you will see what is meant. In that desperate hour when they were slaves and serfs, in bondage in Egypt, the angel of death passed over and spared them, and in that first Passover they were born as a nation by the grace of God. They were redeemed, brought out of bondage and set free. Then, in the marvelous phrasing of Moses, God carried them on eagles' wings and bore them along, upholding them and sustaining them by miraculous interventions on their behalf. (See Exodus 19:4.)

But his goodness and grace were repaid, for the most part, by pride, arrogance, and a self-righteous effort to please him without any genuine conviction of heart. They fell to murmuring, complaining, and grumbling, in constant frustration of God's efforts with them. At last there follows the story of gradually increasing moral failure and of final dispersion in moral bankruptcy and despair.

For centuries they wandered throughout the length and breadth of the earth, preserved as a nation but still in unbelief. Even when they were allowed to go back to Israel and establish themselves as a nation, again they did so in unbelief. But, says Jesus, the hour is coming when by an act of sovereign grace, without any merit on their part, God will bring them back again to the land. This time it will be an hour of mourning and repentance when they will understand at last what God has been wanting to do with them. They will then enter into a time of national health and wholeness and will become the instrument of blessing to all the earth.

If you read carefully the book of Romans you will see that spiritually the same story is told in chapters 5-8. These detail for us the way God has designed to bring men into genuine liberty, genuine joy, and the true excitement of life. In chapters 9-11 of Romans Israel is brought in as the illustration of all this. These chapters trace for us the way God will work with us. When we come to the place of utter spiritual bankruptcy, when we stop thinking we can contribute something of value to God, and begin at last to rest, to rely wholly upon his ability to do everything through us— then we begin to enter into the fullness of life that God has planned for man. This is the meaning of God's dealings with Israel.

Prayer: Lord Jesus, we thank you that at this very moment we may experience your living presence in our hearts. We do not need to wait until some future day in order to know the glory of your presence. We long for the day when earth shall know your presence in power and glory, but in the meantime we are glad we can say with deep personal meaning: "Thine is the kingdom, the power, and the glory." In your name, Amen.

9

A Thief in the Night
Matthew 24:32-44

How can we be sure all this will happen? No doubt you have asked that more than once before now. If you have, you are not the first one to do so. In fact it would be rather strange if you haven't. Even Jesus anticipates a certain degree of honest doubt, for at this point in his discourse (verse 32) he breaks off his description of the last days to give three powerful guarantees that all he has said will actually come to pass.

> "From the fig tree learn its lesson: as soon as its branch becomes tender and puts forth its leaves, you know that summer is near. So also, when you see all these things, you know that he is near, at the very gates."

This is the first guarantee. It is another pattern from nature which illustrates the point he wishes to make. Everyone knows that when the trees begin to put forth their leaves it is an infallible indication that summer is near. Some have misread this to mean that the fig tree is a symbol for the nation Israel and that the Lord means to say that when Israel shows signs of life as a nation that then the end is near. Of course that is perfectly true, but that is not what he is saying here. Luke tells us that he said this not only about the fig tree, but also of "all the trees" (Luke 21:29).

What the Lord means is that as history unfolds and it becomes apparent that the world is heading toward the conditions he describes, then men can be very sure that his coming is near. The trend of world events is the guarantee that he has been telling the truth about the future. History will confirm his predictions as it unfolds. When the world reaches the stage he describes and the possibility of the coming of the Lawless One looms on the horizon of current affairs, then "he is near, at the very gates." We are now nearing the end of two thousand years of history and each man can judge for himself whether or not the world is approaching these events.

The indestructible generation

Then the Lord offers a second guarantee, contained in an often misunderstood statement in verse 34:

"Truly, I say to you, this generation will not pass away till all these things take place."

Many have wondered exactly what he meant by these words. Did he refer to the generation to which he was speaking, i.e., the disciples and their contemporaries? Or did he perhaps mean the generation which would be alive when the events he predicted will begin to be fulfilled? If that is what he meant, he would have been saying that when these events begin they would be completed before the generation would pass. Each of these meanings has been suggested as a possible explanation of his words.

But the truth is, he meant neither of these. Of course, if he meant the disciples' generation then his words have long ago been proved false. And the second explanation involves a very forced and unnatural meaning for the word "this." The only other alternative is that the word "generation" means the Jewish people. "This people will not pass away till all these things take place."

The indestructible people

It is almost certain that this is what the Lord meant, for he used the word "generation" in this very sense in the previous chapter, Matthew 23:33-36. He was speaking in severe and sharp tones to the Pharisees, and he said:

> "You serpents, you brood of vipers, how are you to escape being sentenced to hell? Therefore I send you prophets and wise men and scribes, some of whom you will kill and crucify, and some you will scourge in your synagogues and persecute from town to town, that upon you may come all the righteous blood shed on earth, from the blood of innocent Abel to the blood of Zechariah the son of Barachiah, whom you murdered between the sanctuary and the altar. Truly, I say to you, all this will come upon this generation."

The Lord surely did not mean by this that the Pharisees and their contemporaries would bear the blame for all the injustice of the ages. No, he meant that Israel was the nation chosen to be the instrument of God to teach the whole world what he is like. When Israel failed it became culpable for all the dire results that failure brings. It is the nation which was in view when he uses the term, "this generation."

Throughout twenty centuries of dispersion and persecution a most remarkable demonstration of the truth of the Bible has been the Jewish people and their uncanny ability to survive as an identifiable race. Despite the long centuries of hardship and cruelty they have proved to be an indestructible people. That fact constitutes proof that what Jesus predicts will surely come to pass.

Surer than sunrise

The third assurance Jesus offers is his own infallible promise: "Heaven and earth will pass away, but my words will not pass away" (verse 35). How much value do you give to what he says? This is the One who came to open blind eyes—and he did! He said he would give life to men—and he did! He declared he would give his life as a ransom for many—and he did! He said he would rise again from the dead—and he did! Now he says he will come again— can you believe him?

What is it we count on today as the most dependable thing we know? Is it not the continuity of events? We count on tomorrow's sun to rise, on there being a future. We lay our plans on that basis. But Jesus says that will stop, will pass away, but his words will not. His coming, then, is more certain than the most certain thing we know of. The word by which all things were called into being is the foundation upon which he rests this statement, "my words will not pass away."

Unpredictable timing

At this point in the discourse there comes a definite break. The Lord has completed his outline of the events during the end of the age. He has revealed his *parousia,* his presence on earth, during the entire period of the last days and also the spectacular outshining of his presence to occur at the end. But he has said very little about its beginning. Now, in verses 36-41, he brings that remarkable event before the disciples as the dominant point of emphasis:

"But of that day and hour no one knows, not even the angels of heaven, nor the Son, but the Father only. As were the days of Noah, so will be the coming of the Son of man. For as in those days before the flood they were eating and drinking, marrying and giving in marriage, until the day when Noah entered the ark, and they did not know until the flood came and swept them all away, so will be the coming of the Son of man. Then two men will be in the field; one is taken and one is left. Two women will be grinding at the mill; one is taken and one is left."

As we mentioned in an earlier chapter, some have confused this coming with the glorious manifestation of his presence, described in verse 30. But the first sentence of this section makes clear which aspect of his presence the Lord is describing. He states most forcefully that this coming will be completely unpredictable. "But of the day and hour no one knows, not even the angels of heaven, nor the Son, but the Father only."

This unpredictable element is underscored heavily in the additional warning he gives the disciples in verses 42-44:

"Watch therefore, for you do not know on what day your Lord is coming. But know this, that if the householder had known in what part of the night the thief was coming, he would have watched and would not have let his house be broken into. Therefore you also must be ready; for the Son of man is coming at an hour you do not expect."

It would be impossible for Jesus to use these words if he were referring to the coming in power and great glory. Before that event occurs "the sun will be darkened, and the moon will not give its light, and the stars will fall from heaven, and the powers of the heavens will be shaken." Who could miss that? Who, knowing the Scriptures, would not expect the return of Jesus after such dramatic events? But to his disciples he says, "The Son of man is coming at an hour you do not expect."

This is clearly then his coming as a thief in the night. It is his coming for the church, the unsuspected treasure of earth. He will come to take it to himself, and the world will have no inkling that it is about to occur. As he has just said, we can know that the time is drawing near as we observe the predicted pattern taking shape in the affairs of men. We can see the attitudes that he says will prevail in that day beginning to emerge as the dominant philosophy of the day. But we can never know the day nor the hour. Even the angels do not know, nor did the Son in the time of his earthly limitation, but only the Father.

Top secret

Men seem to display an urgent passion to set dates for the coming of Christ. Several times in history it has been announced that Jesus Christ would return on such and such a date. Some fanatics who believed these reports have even sold their property, donned white robes, and gone out on some hilltop to wait for him to appear. The whole subject of the return of Christ has been cast into disrepute by such foolish actions. God has maintained an inscrutable silence about certain matters and this is one of them. The day and the hour is clearly marked, "Top Secret," just as Jesus told the disciples after the resurrection, "It is not for you to know times or seasons which the Father has fixed by his own authority" (Acts 1:7). The activity Jesus wants to encourage is not date-setting but readiness.

Business as usual

Jesus makes even more forceful this totally unexpected character of his initial coming by comparing it to the days of Noah in verses 37-39:

> "As were the days of Noah, so will be the coming [*parousia*] of the Son of man. For as in those days before the flood they were eating and drinking, marrying and giving in marriage, until the day when Noah entered the ark, and they did not know until the flood came and swept them all away, so will be the coming of the Son of man."

There have been many attempts to make these words, "eating and drinking, marrying and giving in marriage," to indicate signs of evil things in the affairs of men. "Eating" has been taken to mean an increase of gluttony throughout the earth. It is, of course, true that one of the signs of middle age is to grow thick, and tired of it, but this is not a sign of the times! Also, "drinking" has been taken to mark an increase in alcoholism and drunkenness, while "marrying and giving in marriage" has been made to refer to a rocketing divorce rate.

But there is no thought of this in the mind of our Lord. What he is saying is, life will be going on as usual. Men will eat, drink, and marry just as they have always done. It was like that in the days of Noah, before the flood. Life was going on in ordinary fashion. Moral conditions were bad, there was violence and corruption throughout the earth, but they were no worse than they had been for quite some time.

The point our Lord makes is that "they did not know" until the flood came. There was no sense of any coming disaster. This, despite the preaching of Noah for one hundred and twenty years during which he faithfully warned his generation that God would judge the world of that day. And despite the familiar sight of the huge ark that was built a long way from any ocean large enough to float it. Men must have laughed and called him "crazy Noah." But life went on as usual and the first sign of any disaster was the quiet, almost unnoticed removal of a select company from the world of that day.

Noah and his family were told to take the animals and go into the ark. God shut the door of the ark so that Noah and his family, eight people in all, were separated from the world. Then a full week went by and nothing happened. Noah, his family, and all the animals were in the ark for a week and during that time the skies were blue, the sun shone, men went to work in the morning and came home in the evening. Lovers strolled hand in hand as they had done for centuries. Babies cried, men ate and drank and rose up to play, life went on as usual. Then suddenly clouds began to form, the skies darkened, the earth began to heave, the bottom of the sea raised and great tidal waves came crashing across the earth, the skies poured down untold tons of water for forty days and forty nights. All those who lived in the world of that day, "Went down with a bubbly groan, Unwept, unhonored, and unknown."

So, the Lord says, will be the *"parousia,"* the coming as a thief in the night. Jesus Christ will come stealthily, without warning, and a select company will be removed from the earth. That event he plainly describes in verses 40,41: "Then two men will be in the field; one is taken and one is left. Two women will be grinding at the mill; one is taken and one is left."

A selective removal

The event will be highly selective, distinguishing even between two people working side by side. Further, it will be worldwide, for Luke tells us (17:34), "There will be two men in one bed; one will be taken and the other left." While men work in their fields on one side of the earth, others will be asleep in their beds on the other side. But simultaneously, both in the day and in the night, the great removal will occur.

From human experience we feel there is only one way to leave this life. We enter it through the door marked "birth," and

113

we will leave it through the door marked "death." But on the Mount of Transfiguration the Lord showed Peter, James and John that there is another way by which men could go to glory. He was suddenly transfigured before their astonished eyes. His raiment began to glow and he was a different person, yet the same Jesus.

So Paul says in I Corinthians 15:51,52: "We shall not all sleep [die], but we shall all be changed, in a moment, in the twinkling of an eye." It is an event simply unexplainable in natural terms, but there can be no question about the clear language Scripture employs. As Paul told the Thessalonians: "The dead in Christ will rise first; then we who are alive, who are left, shall be caught up together with them in the clouds to meet the Lord in the air" (I Thessalonians 4:16,17).

There are some Bible scholars who take the Lord's words, "one is taken and the other left," in a somewhat different light. They feel the ones taken are not taken to glory but taken in judgment during the tribulation, i.e., killed, while the ones left are left alive to enter into the kingdom following. This, they say, would be more in line with the illustration the Lord uses of Noah's flood where men were swept away by the judgment of the flood.

But several severe objections appear to this opinion. First, no one was left behind in Noah's flood. They were all taken in judgment and there was nothing selective about it. The only ones who survived were Noah and his family who were taken out of the flood before it began. Second, the word the Lord uses for "taken" is a different Greek word from that which is used for the effects of the flood. That is one word, translated, "swept away." Third, the picture the Lord draws is one of sudden, unexpected removal and it is quite a straining of that picture to imagine execution as always occurring in that manner throughout the Tribulation. Fourth, if the Lord is not here describing his coming for the church then we have no description from his lips of that tremendous event. All we would have would be his promise, "I will come again and will take you to myself" (John 14:3).

Because of these objections it is much more plausible to view this passage as our Lord's clear description of his coming "as a thief in the night," accomplishing a silent resurrection and transfiguration which will take the true church out of the judgment of the tribulation, as Noah and his family were taken out of the judgment of the flood.

Keep ready! Watch!

To this vivid description of the silent departure of the church, the Lord immediately adds a word of admonition:

> "Watch therefore, for you do not know on what day your Lord is coming. But know this, that if the householder had known in what part of the night the thief was coming, he would have watched and would not have let his house be broken into. Therefore you also must be ready; for the Son of man is coming at an hour you do not expect."

Notice carefully his argument here. He says that if the householder had known when the thief was coming he would have watched and prevented the robbery. That is, if a man knows he is to be robbed at night, and knows the very hour in which it will take place, he will be ready for the burglar when he comes. No burglar sends a notice ahead of time of his arrival, for if he did he could count on being met by a reception committee. When the robber arrived, the householder would be ready.

So, says Jesus, since you do not know when your Lord is coming, then keep ready all the time. Be always ready. Surely that does not mean we are to gaze skyward all the time, or fold our hands and sit down to wait for him. Some years ago a religious magazine published a cartoon that showed a man standing in a wheat field. The sheaves had been stacked in bundles wait-

115

ing for the harvest. He was standing there with a telescope glued to his eyes looking out to the horizon. Underneath was the caption, "Looking for the coming of the Lord." It suggested that such looking was foolish while the fields were white unto harvest all around, and nothing was being done.

It is very difficult, of course, to keep one eye peeled toward the sky while doing your daily work. But our Lord does not mean this when he says, "Watch!" What does he mean? Clearly one thing he means by this, as highlighted throughout this discourse, is, be not deceived! He has been warning of the deceitfulness of the age. We shall be surrounded by the spurious, the phony, which will nevertheless dazzle us and draw us. If we believe the lies that are part of the great brainwashing campaign behind the philosophy of the world, we shall soon lose our perspective. Life then will get out of focus and we shall become blinded and tragically self-deceived.

The only defense is a continuous, step-by-step, reliance on the truth from God, illuminated to us by an indwelling Spirit. Jesus said, "If you continue in my word, you are truly my disciples, and you will know the truth, and the truth will make you free" (John 8:31,32). That is why we desperately need the Word of God, and the Spirit of God to apply that Word to our daily experience. The only defense against deceit is an obedient ear and a willingness to follow the promptings of the Spirit into an unceasing ministry of loving concern and service, in the name of Jesus Christ. In another place, Jesus said, "Occupy till I come" (Luke 19:13, *KJV*). That means, keep going, keep busy in the strength and purpose of God.

A strange paradox

Many Christians seem to feel that waiting for Christ's coming means that we must behave ourselves lest we should suddenly be caught short by his appearing and be ashamed of what we were doing. But Jesus is no policeman, waiting to surprise us

116

in an unguarded moment. The paradox of the Christian life is that though we look for him to come, yet all the while we are enjoying his presence and experiencing his power. He is coming, and yet he is with us now.

What Jesus wants us to grasp is that these two activities are related. The intensity with which we love his coming is the revelation of the degree to which we are experiencing his presence. The hunger you may feel to see his face is directly proportionate to the present enjoyment you have of his presence. If to you the thought of his coming is a frightening thing, then you know little or nothing of his presence now. But if you do know what it means to live by Christ, if moment by moment with your whole being you are taking from him all that he makes available to you, you will find a longing, a yearning in your heart for his personal coming.

A Christian poetess, Annie Johnson Flint, has put that thought in a wonderful fashion:

> "It is not for a sign we are watching—
> For wonders above and below,
> The pouring of vials of judgment,
> The sounding of trumpets of woe;
> It is not for a Day we are looking,
> Not even the time yet to be
> When the earth shall be filled with God's glory
> As the waters cover the sea;
> It is not for a King we are longing
> To make the world-kingdoms His own;
> It is not for a Judge who shall summon
> The nations of earth to His throne.
>
> Not for these, though we know they are coming;
> For they are but adjuncts of Him,
> Before whom all glory is clouded,
> Besides whom all splendor grows dim.

We wait for the Lord, our Beloved,
Our Comforter, Master, and Friend,
The substance of all that we hope for,
Beginning of faith, and its end;
We watch for our Savior and Bridegroom,
Who loved us and made us His own;
For Him we are looking and longing:
For Jesus, and Jesus alone."*

The great Scottish minister, Horatio Bonar, on one occasion sat with a number of fellow ministers. He said to them, "Do you really expect Jesus Christ to come today?" One by one he went around the circle and put that question to each. And one by one they shook their heads and said, "No, not today." Then without comment he wrote on a piece of paper these words and passed it around:

"Therefore you also must be ready; for the Son of man is coming at an hour you do not expect."

Prayer: Lord Jesus, Thank you that we do not need to wait until some future day to know the glory of your presence, but can experience it during every day we live. But we pray that in this moment of waiting and watching we shall recognize that the strength of our hope is determined by the experience of your present life. Teach us then how to "occupy till you come," in a ministry of loving concern and help to others. In your name, Amen.

*FLINT Poems, "The Lord Himself" Vol. I, Evangelical Publishers. Toronto, Canada. Used by permission.

10

In the Meantime
Matthew 24:45-51

In a small country store in a southern state a black lady came to do her shopping. Two or three young men were standing around passing the time of day, and knowing that she was a Christian, they began to taunt her. "We hear you're expecting Jesus to come back," they said.

"I sure am," she replied brightly.

"Do you really believe he's coming?" they asked.

"Sure as you're born," she answered.

They said, "Well, you'd better hurry home and get ready, he might be on the way!"

She turned and fixed her tormentors with a look. "I don't have to get ready," she said, "I *keep* ready!"

That is exactly the attitude the Lord meant to engender when he said to his disciples, "Watch!" He does not mean, "Keep staring at the sky." He means, "Keep ready at all times." Now to make it perfectly clear what that would involve he goes on to give them three parables, each of which is an exposition of that one word, "Watch!" The first is the parable of the household which tells us that watching means a mutual concern and ministry of the Word to one another. The second is the parable of the ten maidens which makes clear that watching means a dependence on deeper things than mere human resources. And the third is the parable of the talents where we learn that watching means a deliberate investment of life.

Three illustrative parables

It is evident that the Lord has now finished, for the most part, the predictive part of his discourse. Except for a few details concerning the final scene of the judgment of the nations, there are no new events described in the rest of his message. But it is extremely important that we understand these parables, for if we do not understand them we will not watch in the way he expects. And if we do not watch we will be deceived and miss much, if not all, of the exciting possibilities of the present hour. So let us listen carefully to his parable of the household, verses 45-47:

> "Who then is the faithful and wise servant, whom his master has set over his household, to give them their food at the proper time? Blessed is that servant whom his master when he comes will find so doing. Truly, I say to you, he will set him over all his possessions."

This parable is clearly for the instruction of those who are awaiting the Lord's return. The master of the household is gone but he has entrusted certain work to his steward until he returns. That work is primarily a ministry to the rest of the household, and notably, "to give them their food at the proper time." It is clearly addressed to the disciples and to those who will follow in their steps in the ministry of feeding and shepherding the church of Jesus Christ. Doubtless it includes any who have a ministry of teaching: pastors, evangelists, prophets, elders, Sunday School teachers, children's workers and Bible class leaders. It takes in any who have gifts of teaching, whether exercised in a church building or in homes. It includes theological professors, editors of magazines, radio teachers, missionaries, youth workers, and many others.

Give them food!

Since this is the first parable in the series it probably points up the most essential element in the matter of watching. The wise servant is given one major and primary responsibility: to feed the household at the proper time. If this is rightly done, the household will keep watching; if it is neglected, the household will languish and starve, and will not be ready when the Lord returns.

The task, therefore, of any leader within the church is to unfold the message of the Bible. Every pastor should set a loaded table before his congregation, not only that they might eat and grow, but also that they might learn from him how to draw from the Scriptures for themselves the spiritual nourishment they need. The Bible is wonderfully adapted to this purpose: there is milk for the beginner, bread for the more advanced, and strong meat to challenge and feed the mature. It is so designed that when books of the Bible are taught through consecutively they will cover a wide variety of subjects and yet keep truth marvelously in balance.

It is clearly evident, therefore, that the supreme need of the church during this time of waiting for its Lord is Bible study and knowledge. From this all else will flow. The Bible is the revelation of things as they really are. It represents the only truly realistic look at life that is available to man today. It is the only instrument provided by God that is adequate to the task of producing mature, well-adjusted, whole persons. That is the clear claim of II Timothy 3:16,17: "All scripture is inspired by God and profitable for teaching, for reproof, for correction, and for training in righteousness, *that the man of God may be complete, equipped for every good work."*

I am the bread of life

Be careful that you do not conclude from this that the Bible itself is the food for believers. It is not the book but the Lord which the book reveals that is our food. Christ is found in the Scriptures, both Old and New Testaments. But Bible study alone can be most dull and uninteresting if one does not expect the Spirit to take the words and from them cause the living Christ to emerge. That explains why some Bible students are such dull and dry people; they have concentrated on the Word alone, without the Spirit. And yet it is impossible to know the Lord Jesus in the fullness of his being without the revelation of the Word. We cannot neglect the Bible and grow in Christ; but we can grow in the knowledge of Scripture and never feed upon a risen Lord.

The incredible reward

Imagine the joy of that servant when his lord returns and finds him faithfully at the task he assigned him. "Blessed is that servant," says Jesus. The Greek word for "blessed" can also be translated "happy." What a satisfying feeling it will be to know that he did his work well in the eyes of the only one who counts. What shall be done for such a man? What the Lord says next is truly amazing. Listen to it: "Truly, I say to you, he will set him over all his possessions." In another place Jesus said, "You have been faithful over a little, I will set you over much" (Matthew 25:21). This is the invariable rule of the kingdom of God.

When you consider who this master really is, it becomes almost incredible that he should reward this servant by setting him over *all* his possessions. How much is that? Well, Paul wrote in I Corinthians 3:21-23:

"For all things are yours, whether Paul or Apollos or Cephas or the world or life or death or the present or the future, all are yours; and you are Christ's; and Christ is God's."

There is a staggering thought in Paul's letter to the Ephesians which sums all this up in the phrase, "the unsearchable riches of Christ." Who can tell what boundless opportunities, what indescribable adventures of service, what fabulous vistas of challenge, are involved in a phrase like that? Surely one thing is clear: the commitment and labor required to fulfill the ministry of teaching which the Lord has left for us to do will not be worthy to be compared with what shall belong to a "faithful and wise servant" when the Lord returns.

The unfaithful servant

But unfortunately not every servant of the Lord proves to be wise and faithful. With the utter candor that characterizes him, Jesus gives the negative side of the picture in verses 48-51:

"But if that wicked servant says to himself, 'My master is delayed,' and begins to beat his fellow servants, and eats and drinks with the drunken, the master of that servant will come on a day when he does not expect him and at an hour he does not know, and will punish him, and put him with the hypocrites; there men will weep and gnash their teeth."

It is evident that this servant has the same ministry committed to him as the first one. He, too, is expected "to give them their food at the proper time." The same storehouse of the Word is at his disposal so that he too can feed the hungry of the household whenever they need it. The health and welfare of the household is his responsibility and depends upon his faithful ministry.

But this servant is different. When his lord does not come as soon as he expects, he says to himself, "My master is delayed." There is more than a hint here that the return of the Lord Jesus will be delayed far beyond the expectations of men. The apostles expected him in the first century, but he did not come. Now many centuries have gone by, and the effect of that long delay has been what the Lord here predicts. Many who claim to be his servants have given up the hope of his return. The former bishop of the Episcopal Church, James Pike, himself one who had given up such a hope, stated that "only 24% of Episcopalians, by survey, believe it."* The effect of that lost hope is immediately apparent. The servant, says the Lord, begins to beat his fellow servants, mistreat them, criticize and complain continually, neglect his ministry, and indulge his appetites to the full. It is a vivid picture of what happens, in one degree or another, when the expectation of the Lord's return is abandoned. There is a precise sequence of failure that can be traced. First, the hope of the Lord's return grows weak and eventually is lost. Because of this there is little motivation to the ministry of feeding the household, and therefore it is neglected. When the Word is not taught the people grow spiritually weak, and therefore full of weakness and carnality. This then manifests itself in quarreling, injustices, and excesses of every sort, in which the servant responsible for the feeding also joins.

It should be obvious from this that the fact of Christ's return is more important as a doctrine of the church than may at first appear. As we have already seen, it is an indicator of the degree to which the Lord's present indwelling life is being experienced. If there is little desire for his appearing, there is little concern to walk in the strength of his life. When the hope of the Lord's return crumbles, then it is already apparent that the experience

*Life Magazine, April 29, 1969.

of his present life has largely ceased, if it existed at all. That is why the Lord lays such stress upon this and underscores it as the primary cause for the neglect of Bible teaching and the subsequent weakness of the church.

But though the servant has given up on the lord's return, that does not prevent the lord from returning. Suddenly he appears at an hour which the servant does not know and at a time when he does not expect him. Undoubtedly this will be one of those occasions when the servant will say, "Lord, Lord, have I not done mighty works in your name?" There may indeed be other things he has done which he felt would be impressive to the lord if he returned. But it is all to no avail. He has specifically not done the one thing the lord required of him. He has been faithless to his commission. Therefore he shall be punished and put where he belongs—with the hypocrites! He is himself a hypocrite, for he has assumed the name of a faithful servant of the lord, but has proved false to his trust.

It is obvious from what our Lord says of this man, that he has never been a true servant at all. His destiny is to be put in the place where men will weep and gnash their teeth. Further on, in chapter 25, verse 30, the Lord describes that place as "outer darkness." It is a place of frustration and defiance. Men weep because of their lost opportunities; they gnash their teeth out of bitter rage and defiance. It is not a pleasant picture, but let us remember, it is the Lord Jesus Christ who thus describes it to us.

A demoralized household

The Lord has made crystal clear by this parable that it is a very serious thing to fail in feeding the household of God. It is not because the man's personal failure is so bad, it is because his failure has a demoralizing effect upon the household. This has been most apparent in the church. One of the haunting problems in the church today is its identity crisis. In many places it seems to have lost the sense of what it was intended to be. Instead of a body, with each one "members one of another" and ministering to one another in love and concern, it has become an organization operating various programs. Paul wrote to the Galatians, "Bear one another's burdens, and so fulfill the law of Christ" (Galatians 6:2). But today's Christians often touch each others' lives on only the most superficial basis, and do not want to hear another's problems because they "don't want to get involved."

This widespread ignorance of the church's true nature is directly traceable to a lack of systematic Bible teaching. Many passages in the New Testament epistles plainly detail the true nature of the church. Its "body life" is clearly described and illustrated from actual experience. Its supernatural endowment with spiritual gifts as the basis for all its ministry is described in half a dozen places. Its unique power, deriving from the presence of an indwelling and active Lord, is set before us again and again. The way to the consistent exercise of spiritual power, making its impact upon a decadent society, is detailed in many places.

Results of biblical ignorance

But how much does the average Christian know of this? The blunt answer is: scarcely anything! In church after church the congregation hardly knows that the passages exist, let alone having a clear understanding of them. The degree of biblical illiteracy prevalent in American churches is beyond belief. And the widespread effect, visible everywhere, is a powerless, quarreling, materialistic church whose knowledge of its Lord's living presence is almost nil, and whose hope of his soon return has long ago burned out into gray embers.

The cause for this sterile mediocrity is, says Jesus, faithless and wicked servants who have never assumed or have given up the task of feeding the household at the proper time. He views this failure with the greatest solemnity. There is a sobering word from Paul in I Corinthians 3:17: "If any one destroys God's temple, God will destroy him. For God's temple is holy, and that temple you are." Consequently we should not be surprised to hear Jesus say that when the master of the house returns he will confront the faithless servant and "will punish him, and put him with the hypocrites; there men will weep and gnash their teeth."

The secrets of the heart

In both of these cases, that of the faithful and that of the faithless servant, it is evident that the return of Jesus Christ simply reveals what men have been all the time. "Each man's work will become manifest," says Paul, "for the Day will disclose it" (I Corinthians 3:13). The truly shocking thing about that is that what we are proved to be in that Day, we will be forever! What we have been in the secret places of the heart through life must now be displayed as our true self through eternity.

Thus the Lord desires to emphasize to us that the present time is an exceedingly precious commodity. It is given to us to redeem. Dr. Helmut Thielicke,* a noted German author, points out that on New Year's Eve we learn something about time we can never learn in any other way. Then we look at our watch or clock quite differently from any other day of our lives. Usually we glance at our watch in order to see what time we should be at a certain place, or whether we are going to make an appointment on time. But on New Year's Eve we suddenly look at it, not in order to move ourselves, but because we become aware of the fact that time itself is moving.

Our personal time line

Dr. Thielicke says that then we can almost hear the stream of time beginning to murmur as it drops over the dam of that strange midnight hour. We become aware of the fact that we are

*How the World Began, Fortress Press, Philadelphia.

not living an endless repetitive cycle, but we are moving on a straight line of time, and we can never retrace it. The reason we do not experience this more frequently is because our clocks are round; that is, if we haven't finished something by six o'clock this morning we know that the hands of the clock will come around to six o'clock tonight, and we can get it done by then. Or by six o'clock tomorrow night. We suffer, therefore, from the illusion that time is repeating itself.

But on New Year's Eve we discover otherwise. We become quite aware, as the midnight hour approaches, that time is moving continually on and that we can never go back, that what we have been will unalterably remain, forever. It can never be changed. We can never retrace our steps nor refill the contents of the past with something either better or worse. It remains exactly what it was. Perhaps last year we made a wrong decision or got married (the two are not necessarily linked) or entered into some new project or achieved some goal. Whatever it was, that has now become an unchangeable part of our destiny, our lot. It is irrevocably the same; it can never be changed. God's grace has moved him to bear certain effects of our misdeeds himself, but they remain for him to bear and are never dissipated into nothingness. If that grace is rejected, there is no escape.

A final New Year's Eve

This is what the sudden intervention of Jesus Christ into human affairs seems to be: a final New Year's Eve midnight hour when men will become aware that life has been lived and it is whatever it is and will never be any different. No one can go back and change it. That leaves us facing an inevitable question: How long have you lived? "Oh," you say, "I am (so many) years old." No, you cannot answer in those terms. The only part of life that can be called living is the time you have been watching for your Lord's return in the strength of his abiding life. All else is death.

The great missionary to Africa, C. T. Studd, summed up the truth in a little couplet:

> "Only one life, 'twill soon be past,
> Only what's done for Christ will last."

Now let us ask it again: How long have you lived? How much of your life will abide the day of his coming? Whatever is not gold, silver, or precious stones, coming from the activity of his life in you, is nothing more than wood, hay and stubble. When are you going to start living? You have only today!

Prayer: Father, keep us from the folly of dreaming away our days in a fruitless endeavor to satisfy only the fancies of our spirit and the appetites of our bodies. Deliver us from the bondage of things. Teach us how to feed upon the Word of truth, and to walk continually in that truth, manifesting the splendor of your life in us. In Jesus' name, Amen.

11

The Wise and the Foolish
Matthew 25:1-13

The second parable

Weddings never go out of style. They are as old fashioned as the race and as modern as today's newspaper. There is something fresh and beautiful about each one for we never seem to get over the excitement of watching two lives become one. At most weddings a lot of fuss is made over the bride and groom, but no one pays much attention to the attendants. Not so with Jesus. He chooses to use a wedding scene as a parable, to illustrate further what he means by the command, "Watch!" He doesn't even mention the bride and only incidentally the bridegroom. His attention is focused on ten young ladies who were invited to the marriage.

Do not pay any attention to the chapter division which occurs at this point in the biblical text. It is quite apparent that the Lord is still talking about the unexpectedness of his return for the church, and of the need to keep watching for it. This is made evident by his use of "Then" to introduce the parable of the ten maidens. "Then the kingdom of heaven shall be compared to ten maidens," etc. It is at the time of his coming as a thief in the night before the Great Tribulation, when he shall appear on a day when he does not expect him and at an hour he does not know. And when he finishes the story of the ten maidens the Lord adds again, "Watch therefore, for you know neither the day nor the hour."

Let us now join him as he relates this story to the disciples on the Mount of Olives.

> "Then the kingdom of heaven shall be compared to ten maidens who took their lamps and went to meet the bridegroom. Five of them were foolish, and five were wise. For when the foolish took their lamps, they took no oil with them; but the wise took flasks of oil with their lamps. As the bridegroom was delayed, they all slumbered and slept. But at midnight there was a cry, 'Behold, the bridegroom! Come out to meet him.' Then all those maidens rose and trimmed their lamps" (Matthew 25:1-7).

That is not the whole story but it is enough of it to serve as an introduction. The background is an eastern wedding in which the bridegroom, rather than the bride, is the center of attention. In Oriental weddings it is the bridegroom who bears all the expense of the wedding (which seems a bit fairer than our system where the poor father of the bride has to foot the bill for giving up his daughter to another man!) and thus has the prime spot. Weddings were always held at night and it was customary for the bridegroom to go to the house of the bride and take her to the wedding. As they walked through the streets they would be joined by guests at various places along the route. Our Lord's story of the ten maidens is the story of such a group, waiting for the bridegroom.

There are five movements in this story as the Lord tells it. Let us remember that it was intended for those who live in the intervening time between our Lord's first coming and his second. It will be of value to us only as we permit it to be autobiographical, if we recognize ourselves somewhere in the story. It is clearly intended to describe an element of watching that is vital and essential. If we miss the point of it we shall be unable to watch for his coming as he desires.

A common expectation

The first movement of the story is one of a common expectation. Here is a body of people who are waiting for someone. Life seems to be made up of a great deal of waiting. When we are little we wait to grow up. When we are half-grown we wait to get out on our own. When we are in college we wait to get married. When we get married we wait for children, and so it goes. One of the characteristics of life which makes it worth living is this note of waiting. There must be something beyond, something worth waiting for. Otherwise life can become terribly colorless and purposeless.

These maidens were waiting for the coming of the bridegroom. In terms of the Lord's ultimate message, they were waiting for the coming of Jesus Christ. These maidens represent, therefore, those who are convinced that the end of the age will come just as Jesus describes it. They are not deluded by highly colored dreams of an earthly utopia which will be brought about by man's wisdom and skill. They believe in a golden age, but they do not believe that age will ever come by the efforts of men. They are persuaded that only the return of Jesus Christ can accomplish that end, and they are hopeful that his coming will be very soon.

Surely at this point in our study of the Olivet Discourse, most of the readers of this book will represent such a group. We have been listening to the words of God's greatest Prophet. We have heard what he predicts and understood the pattern that he says will prevail as the age draws to a close. We are convinced that history will end at the feet of this One who will come flaming in glory from the heavens to astonish a deluded world. We are, therefore, sharers with these ten maidens in a common expectation of the coming of the Bridegroom.

Wise and foolish

But the second movement of the parable is one of division, of a divided procedure:

> "Five of them were foolish, and five were wise. For when the foolish took their lamps, they took no oil with them; but the wise took flasks of oil with their lamps."

Though this group is united in its expectation it is quite divided in the way it conducts its waiting. Five maidens have brought along extra oil, and five have not. This does not represent a division between good and bad, but, as Jesus says, between the wise and the foolish. Someone has said there are only two kinds of people in the world: the righteous and the unrighteous; but the classifying is always done by the righteous! That is all too humanly true. But here there is no moral division intended. In their expectation of the coming bridegroom they are all equally sincere and devoted. The only difference is, five of them felt it would be wise to provide some extra oil.

This proves ultimately to be the most significant part of this story. Yet to the five foolish maidens it represented only a trivial difference which was as nothing compared with the fact that they were unitedly waiting for the bridegroom's coming. They were all agreed on the importance of oil and were all using it for its proper purpose—the giving of light. The only slight difference was that some felt more was needed than others.

What the oil represents we shall see in a moment, but it is certainly evident that the wise and the foolish are still with us. Despite our agreement in desiring the bridegroom to come, and our conviction that history will end as Jesus describes it, nevertheless, there are doubtless some reading this who will prove in the end to be wise, and others will be revealed as foolish, lacking the essential for waiting till the Lord returns. If this parable has any message at all for us it is that we determine what that essential is.

Seemingly all would have gone well for the whole ten if the bridegroom had come when expected. But the third movement of the story introduces an element of delay:

> "As the bridegroom was delayed, they all slumbered and slept. But at midnight there was a cry, 'Behold, the bridegroom! Come out to meet him.'"

No explanation is given for what delayed the bridegroom. This seems to be another hint from the Lord that his absence would be long extended, as has certainly proved to be the case. It was this protracted delay of the bridegroom which constituted an unexpected demand on the part of the ten maidens for more oil. At any rate, the story describes how all ten grew weary of waiting and fell fast asleep.

There are many interpreters who view this as suggesting negligence on the part of the maidens. But there is no hint of rebuke or disapproval expressed by the Lord for this sleeping. And the wise slept as well as the foolish! It was, therefore, a perfectly natural and right thing to do under the circumstances. It was night and therefore it was impossible to do any work. It was also a festive occasion, and their only purpose for being there was to wait for the bridegroom. So when his coming was delayed they grew drowsy and it was only natural that they would drop off to sleep.

But this is highly suggestive, for it indicates the awareness of Jesus that watching does not mean unceasing, conscious, anticipation of his return. We are not to be continually peering up into the heavens like an air-raid sentry on duty. Nor are we to be forever meeting and singing, "Is It the Crowning Day?" or discussing the Lord's return. Such meetings are helpful and needed, because of the human tendency to forget, but what our Lord is indicating is that watching also allows time for normal activities. Money must be earned, investments looked into, food must be cooked, babies washed, school lessons studied, weddings held, and funerals attended—all the usual activities of life must go on.

While these wise and foolish maidens were sleeping, their thoughts were diverted for the time being from the coming of the bridegroom. Thus while we are engaged in the normal activities of life there is no need to feel guilty because we have not been thinking of the Lord's return. There is nothing at all wrong about this, it is as it should be. We have not failed to watch because we have been busy doing natural and necessary things. These maidens were waiting for the bridegroom's coming even while they slept. There was a sense of imminence when they went out, yet a perfectly proper activity took their attention for a time.

Here comes the bridegroom!

But suddenly there is a cry of warning, "Behold! the bridegroom! Come out to meet him." It may well be that the ten had even posted a sentry to warn them when the bridegroom came, or it may be that the bridegroom was preceded by someone sent for that purpose. At any rate the cry is sounded and all ten of the maidens are wakened. Again it is clearly evident that the problem which would soon confront them did not arise out of the fact that they had fallen asleep. They are awake in plenty of time to meet the bridegroom.

Many times we are, like these, called back to an awareness of the Lord's imminent return by events of the day, or some realization that time is short. We are often made aware that the grind and routine of life was never intended to go on that way forever. And certainly one day the awakening will come not through events but the actual cry, it may be, of the returning Lord himself. Paul tells us that when he comes for the church it will be with a shout, and that shout may be these electrifying words, "Behold, the Bridegroom!"

Inadequate resources

The fourth movement of the story brings a crisis. In it is revealed the wisdom of the wise and the foolishness of the foolish:

> "Then all those maidens rose and trimmed their lamps. And the foolish said to the wise, 'Give us some of your oil, for our lamps are going out.' But the wise replied, 'Perhaps there will not be enough for us and for you; go rather to the dealers and buy for yourselves.'"

To the consternation of the foolish, they find their lamps are flickering, guttering, about to go out. The long delay has used up the oil and they have no more. They make appeal to the wise: "Give us some of your oil." The reply of the wise indicates that oil is not something that can be borrowed or loaned. Whatever it may represent, it is an individual matter. We have all felt something of this in some crisis hour when we have found our resources unequal to the demand. We see someone else who is going through the same thing, and he appears unmoved and calm, well able to take the pressure. We may long to borrow some of his strength, but it is impossible. In such an hour each has what he has and nothing more.

So with these five foolish maidens. Their oil is gone and to their dismay they discover their need and there is a panicky rush to get more. But our Lord moves right on in the story, and the final movement of this parable is one of denial:

> "And while they went to buy, the bridegroom came, and those who were ready went in with him to the marriage feast; and the door was shut. Afterward the other maidens came also, saying, 'Lord, Lord, open to us.' But he replied, 'Truly, I say to you, I do not know you.' Watch therefore, for you know neither the day nor the hour."

When the foolish finally arrived, the door was shut. Are we not surprised at that? Many will probably feel that these five were unjustly treated. Why should they not be allowed into the wedding, even if they were a few moments late? But there is no vindictiveness in this shut door. We must be careful that we do not impose our faulty judgments into this matter. What the Lord did was right, and we must be careful to look diligently for those clues that will help us learn why he takes such action as this. There is even a note of sorrow in these words, "I do not know you." Our Lord's words are a faithful, honest revelation of something that had been true all along. Weddings are no place for strangers. Only the friends of the family are permitted to come. So to these five foolish maidens the door is shut for the Lord says, "Truly, I say to you, I do not know you."

The meaning of oil

With these revealing words from the Lord we can now discover what the oil signifies. Obviously it was lack of an adequate supply of oil which caused these foolish maidens to be met with the words, "I do not know you." They did, of course, have some oil when they began but it was not enough. Oil, in the Old Testament, is frequently used as a symbol of the Holy Spirit. Kings and priests were anointed with oil as a sign of their consecrated (and, supposedly, Spirit-filled) lives. Zechariah the prophet was shown a vision of a great golden lampstand with two olive trees standing beside it. The trees dripped oil into the bowls of the lampstand, and Zechariah was told: "Not by might, nor by power, but by my Spirit, says the LORD of hosts" (Zechariah 4:6). The oil symbolized the Spirit of God by which the light of testimony could be maintained in the hour of darkness.

Some ministry of the Spirit is then in view. The supreme ministry of the Spirit is to impart to men the knowledge of Jesus Christ. In John 16:13,14, Jesus said of him:

> "When the Spirit of truth comes, he will guide you into all the truth; for he will not speak on his own authority, but . . . will declare to you the things that are to come. He will glorify me, for he will take what is mine and declare it to you."

The Spirit's task then is to take the Word of God and through it to reveal Jesus Christ. But there are levels of such revelation. There is even a Spirit-born ministry of the word to those who are not true Christians. Jesus revealed this too. "When he comes, he will convince the world of sin and of righteousness and of judgment" (John 16:8). Here is a ministry of the Holy Spirit available to anyone who will seek in the Scriptures to know the truth. But it is designed to take them deeper, into a fuller and permanent relationship that will involve the imparting of divine life.

Halfway is not enough

The great danger is that in exposure to the truth of Scripture, in the knowledge of its teaching, we should become satisfied with an intellectual portrait of Christ instead of a living Lord. It is possible to know much doctrine but never to know the Lord. This is the problem with the foolish maidens, who represent those who gladly take enough of the oil of the Spirit to give them immediate help in their problems, or some release from fear or guilt, but who never go on to a surrender of the will to the authority of Jesus Christ.

The foolish, then, are those who reckon no deeper than a superficial knowledge of scriptural truth. They look only for moral enlightenment or for comfort in some hour of uncertainty and doubt. They read to gain reassurance when life seems to be a senseless tangle of threads without apparent purpose. They believe in the Bible but not in the Lord of the Bible. But faith must go deeper than doctrine. Orthodox knowledge is worthless unless it leads to the surrender of self. God freely lights a lamp of knowledge for all who want to know the truth of revelation, but what Jesus indicates here is that there is a deeper level of commitment to the Spirit which is essential to meet the unexpected demands life will thrust at us.

The wise have found that deeper level. They have an extra reservoir of oil which continually feeds the flame of life, never letting it falter or gutter out in darkness, undergirding them in every hour of stress, of pressure or disaster, keeping them firm and steady in the midst of the buffeting pressures of life. They have found a friend who sticks closer than a brother. They have a hidden supply of the mystic oil that lights the flame of life despite the circumstances, and the greater the pressure the brighter the light shines.

Perhaps a personal experience will illustrate this. I called on a man in the hospital once, a Christian of many years' standing. I found him unable to talk, sitting up in bed, his body wasted away to a skeleton. He was unable to move a muscle, even to lift his arms or turn his head. The best he could do in the way of talking was to utter a few guttural sounds. I asked him if he would like me to read the Scripture to him and he nodded his head. As I read I watched his eyes. As the marvelous words from passages in Isaiah began to sink into his ears there came a flame into his eyes, a light such as never shone on land or sea. Before we finished I could see in that emaciated body the glory of a flame burning, unquenchable, inexhaustible, fed by the oil of the Spirit, a flame that could never be put out.

Renounce or risk!

Perhaps you are saying, "I'll get along as long as I have my friends and my church." But what if they are taken away? What if you are shipped out to some remote post somewhere, surrounded by 20th century pagans who have committed themselves to seek nothing but the satisfaction of their immediate lusts? What will happen to you then? What if you are transferred to another city and you cannot find a church that ministers to your needs? What if you are confined to bed with a long-term illness, and you must lie there day after unyielding day with little opportunity to speak with others about the things of faith? Or, what is even more likely, what if imperceptibly, despite the eagerness you show now and the earnestness with which you read Scripture or go to church, you begin to drift and gradually are drawn back into the great cold indifference of the deluded masses?

If something like that happens it will do no good to say to another, "Give me of your oil." That cannot be done. Every impartation of the Spirit's power to an individual is marked "Nontransferable." He cannot share it with anyone else. It has been said that there are only two ways to take a thing seriously: either to renounce it or to risk everything upon it. Is this not what Jesus meant when he said, "Whoever would save his life will lose it, and whoever loses his life for my sake will find it" (Matthew 16:25)?

There are some who want a third choice, who are continually seeking to make a partial commitment, who try to find a compromise arrangement with God in which they may subscribe to the truth of Scripture but refuse to let it change their activities or their attitudes. That third alternative simply does not exist. That is what Jesus is saying here. That is why he says plainly to the foolish maidens, "Truly, I say to you, I do not know you." The end shows them for what they are. The door is shut, both to the unbeliever who never tried to get in and to the foolish person who never took God seriously.

Prayer: Lord, how many of us are burning the candle of our life on the shallow reservoir of Scriptural knowledge but have never struck deeper? How many of us are holding you at arm's length concerning specific matters and yet priding ourselves upon our orthodoxy and our Christian faith? Save us from this folly. Bring us into that wonderful experience of finding a flame that can never be put out. In your name, Amen.

12

Living Dangerously
Matthew 25:14-30

Parables can be as exciting and challenging as detective stories. Even more so, for in the end they turn out to be dealing with real life, while detective stories can be pretty farfetched. But parables, like detective stories, are filled with half-hidden truths and secret meanings and yet with clues to these secrets scattered liberally throughout. Parables are God's exciting way of challenging us to a mystery hunt, and the treasure we are after is a new insight into the nature of life which will enrich us in a thousand ways if we act upon it once it is discovered.

The third parable

The parable of the talents is the last in a series of three which Jesus gave his disciples to illustrate what he meant by the command, "Watch!" Its opening words link it to the same time period as the first two, and it reflects the same basic pattern of a master who goes away and leaves a certain company to fulfill a task till he returns. Here is the introduction to it from Matthew 25:14-18:

"For it will be as when a man going on a journey called his servants and entrusted to them his property; to one he gave five talents, to another two, to another one, to each according to his ability. Then he went away. He who had received the five talents went at once and traded with them; and he made five talents more. So also, he who had the two talents made two talents more. But he who had received the one talent went and dug in the ground and hid his master's money."

Interpreting the parable

In many ways this is a deeply puzzling parable. The central question, of course, is: What do the talents represent? There is a common, but quite shallow, understanding of this parable that it teaches the need for us to put our natural gifts to work for God. Someone says, "I play the piano, and I want to devote that talent to the Lord." Another says, "I think I have a gift for speaking (or teaching, or making money, etc.,) and I would like to develop that talent and devote it to Christ."

But when we think of the parable in this way we are being misled by the modern meaning of talent. To us the word means ability—a natural gift which we possess. But it definitely did not mean that in biblical times. The disciples thought of this word as a definite amount of money. The talent was a specific weight of silver, worth about a thousand dollars. Though it was a definite amount of money in the story the Lord told, yet it represents something other than money in our lives. We shall see in a moment why it cannot represent the natural gifts we possess. But the major question before us is: What has the Lord given to us to invest, which corresponds with the talents given to the servants in the parable?

A life or death matter

Another easy pitfall we must avoid is to interpret this parable as though it dealt only with the matter of ultimate rewards for service. This concept often accompanies the idea that the talents represent natural gifts. We must use our natural gifts to the full for Christ, we are told, lest in the end we lose our reward, though of course we will not lose our salvation. But salvation is the very thing that is at stake in this parable. It is the ultimate destiny of a professed servant of Christ which is the issue. The last line of the story makes that crystal clear. Of the man with one talent, the returned master says, "Cast the worthless servant into the outer darkness; there men will weep and gnash their teeth." The final scene therefore reveals that the worthless servant was not really a Christian at all.

So it is apparent that the talents are not distributed only to true believers but are given to false and true alike, that is, any who in any sense recognize the authority of the Lord and who claim to be his servants. But what is done with the talents distributed is an exceedingly vital issue. The destiny of the individual hangs on the matter. It is a question of life or death.

Once again, we must treat this parable autobiographically. We must see that it is intended for us. In Mark's account of this same parable (Mark 13:32-37), the Lord says, "What I say to you [disciples] I say to all: Watch." The parable is addressed to any who have any interest or conviction that what Jesus describes as the outcome of history will actually take place. To each one the Lord has distributed one or more talents. We are either trading with it or burying it in the ground. As we read the parable we must face, in terrible loneliness, that central issue.

Now, having gotten our perspective straight, we turn to the inevitable question: "What are the talents, in our experience?" There are several clues given to us in the account which will guide us in this search. We shall discover and assess them one by one.

Clue #1

The first clue is found in the opening verse, "For it will be as when a man going on a journey called his servants and entrusted to them his property." The last two words are the key: "his property." That is another term for the talents which are distributed. They are the Lord's property, God's property. They are then, not something which man can give, but something which God alone controls. The talents are not distributed, like natural gifts, to all men freely, but are given only to those who in some fashion have the relationship of a servant to the Lord. To them he is willing to distribute his property.

Clue #2

The second clue is found in the next verse, "to one he gave five talents, to another two, to another one, to each according to his ability." Again, the last phrase is extremely helpful. Here we learn that the talents are clearly not natural abilities but are actually distributed on the basis of natural ability. To one man the lord gave five talents because he was a man of great natural ability, he had many gifts. To another he gave two talents because he was not as gifted as the first, and to the third man he only gave one talent because he had few natural abilities. Whatever the talents may be, one thing is certainly clear: they are not natural abilities. Rather, the number of talents given is determined by the number of natural gifts possessed.

Clue #3

The third clue is not stated in the text but is clearly implied. It is the unspoken implication that the lord expected these servants to invest the talents he distributed in such a way as to produce gain. The talent, then, is something that can be invested, be risked, with the possibility of producing gain or loss. The decision to risk is wholly the servant's. He can choose to take this risk, as the first two servants did, or he can utterly refuse to do so, as the third one did.

Clue #4

The fourth clue is likewise implied. It is that the investment must be made wholly for the benefit of the absent lord. The talent is not given to the servant for his own use. It remains the property of his absent lord and if it is risked it must be on the lord's behalf. There is no promise made to the servants that they will share in any way in whatever profits may be made. They have no right to deduct a broker's percentage. As far as the servant could see, all the loss would be his, all the profit would be the lord's. The lord alone would benefit by this transaction, if anyone would.

The riddle solved

Let us now sum up these four clues and ask ourselves a question. What do we professed Christians have which is God's peculiar property, which comes to us on the basis of natural ability, which requires a risk on our part, and the risk appears to benefit only the Lord and not ourselves? Can you answer that?

Well, look at it this way. Having certain natural abilities, what do you then look for? Recognizing that you have a particular gift, what do you then seek? Is it not an opportunity to use that gift? Do we not all look for such opportunities, young and old alike? As we grow up and feel our powers developing, do we not then look for opportunities to use them? And the more talents we feel we have the more we look for occasions for expression.

So the talents of the parable are to us golden moments of opportunity. Now let us test that to see if it fulfills the qualifications we have discovered and agrees with all the clues.

Is it not apparent at once that opportunities for the exercise of natural gifts are God's peculiar privilege to bestow or with-hold? Who of us, remembering the struggle to express our-selves along some line of natural ability, has not realized that it was beyond our final control whether the opportunity to do so would come or not? Who is not aware of what we call the "lucky breaks" that life occasionally brings us? Or who has not been defeated and discouraged by what we call "bad breaks" when suddenly those opportunities we sought were removed from us? Who governs all this, ultimately? Can we not agree that they are something which God alone gives? They are his property.

It is equally obvious that such opportunities come on the basis of how many natural gifts we possess. Every day we see examples of many-gifted people who seem to abound in opportu-nities to demonstrate what they can do. For those somewhat less gifted the opportunities seem to come less often. And we're all familiar with the Cinderella-type who may have a once-in-a-lifetime opportunity to step into the limelight and display the hid-den talent he or she may have. Thus we can see that the oppor-tunities are given on the basis of natural gifts. So strongly do we sense this that we sometimes say it is the gift which creates the opportunity. But experience does not support that.

Making investments

But it is the third and fourth qualifications which mark an opportunity as equivalent to the biblical talent. Opportunities to display gifts come to all kinds of people, Christian or not; but those opportunities which involve the possibility of gain to Christ come only to professed Christians. Such opportunities are moments of decision when we must choose to play it safe and get what we can for ourselves, or risk our reputation or even our life in order that God may have what he wants. They are hours of fateful decision when we cast the die of our lives for ulti-mate good or evil, though at the moment the only question we may face is, "Will this give me what I want, or will it only make

147

possible for Jesus Christ to do what he wants to do through me?"

These moments can occur when we are confronted with moral choices. "Should I yield to my passions to do this thing I know is wrong, and thus satisfy myself and my urging friends; or should I refuse it, be true to what God wants of me, and perhaps lose my friends and certainly the immediate satisfaction of my lusts?" "Should I accept this new promotion, involving as it does certain questionable business ethics; or should I pass up, for my conscience' sake, the possibility of some new furniture and a better car which the increase in salary would buy?"

Or perhaps there is no moral issue involved, but only the question of where our gifts are to be exercised. "Should I respond to this inner urge to invest my life as a social worker in a slum area for Christ's sake; or should I play it safe and continue my present plans to be a rich lawyer?" "Should I take the time to teach this home Bible class with its life-changing possibilities; or should I go on reserving each Tuesday night for bowling with my friends?" "Should I get involved with my neighbor's seemingly endless problems and try to help her find the strength from God that she needs; or should I forget it and use the time to read, and study, and pray?"

Time for acounting

The God-given opportunities which the talents represent are clearly part of each professed Christian's life. They are distributed to each, according to his ability. But inevitably there will be an accounting. Jesus describes it for us in verses 19-21:

> "Now after a long time the master of those servants came and settled accounts with them. And he who had received the five talents came forward, bringing five talents more, saying, 'Master, you delivered to me five talents; here I have made five

talents more.' His master said to him, 'Well done, good and faithful servant; you have been faithful over a little, I will set you over much; enter into the joy of your master.'"

This first man has gained a one hundred percent return. In terms of the application of this parable to our lives it means that he made full use of his opportunities, not for his own advancement but for his Lord's. He put first the kingdom of God and his righteousness. He made each crucial decision about the investment of his natural ability, not ultimately to profit himself but that the work of Christ might be advanced. He risked the possibility of loss to himself. He took the chance that he might never have the place of prominence, influence, or power which he had wanted, but deliberately invested his opportunity along a line that would give God what he wanted: to bind up the broken-hearted, comfort the fatherless, set at liberty the captives, and proclaim the gospel to the poor.

Christ's "well done"

To this man, whose God-given powers were all at Christ's disposal, not in an empty commitment of word only but in actual deed, Jesus says, "Well done, good and faithful servant." Obviously Jesus Christ would never say "well done" unless it had indeed been well done. This is not empty praise, made meaningless by being spoken to everyone alike, regardless of how well or poorly he has done. Then the Lord sets him over much, which in the estimation of Christ must be a great deal indeed, and adds, "Enter into the joy of your master."

What is that joy? In the book of Hebrews it is said of Jesus, "who for the joy that was set before him endured the cross, despising the shame, and is seated at the right hand of the throne of God" (Hebrews 12:2). It is the joy of accomplishment, the joy of achieving the results for which blood, sweat, and tears have been shed; the shouting joy of having satisfied the heart of God. It is an eternal joy, not passing in a moment as do our times of exultation, but remaining fresh and glorious forever.

Jesus continues the story of the final accounting:

> "And he also who had the two talents came forward, saying, 'Master, you delivered to me two talents; here I have made two talents more.' His master said to him, Well done, good and faithful servant; you have been faithful over a little, I will set you over much; enter into the joy of your master."

The man with two talents had gained two talents more. Is that fifty percent? No, that is one hundred percent, too. That means that to the limits of his ability he, too, had chosen to put Christ's cause first. He was not naturally as able as the other man but he was equally committed. He had risked loss to himself that his Lord's work might prosper. To him, therefore, the Lord says, "Well done, good and faithful servant; you have been faithful over a little, I will set you over much; enter into the joy of your master." There is not one syllable of difference between what the Lord says to the man with two talents and what he said to the man with five!

Perhaps before we go on to view the accounting of the third man, it would be well to pause to answer a question that may be haunting many. What are the additional talents gained by the two men when they invested the talents they were given on behalf of their master? These first two men each had doubled the talents they were given. What do the additional talents represent? Certainly if the talents given represented opportunities then would not the talents gained represent the same? But in the second case, opportunities on a different level, in a higher realm. If the talents given represent opportunities to invest natural gifts, then very likely the talents gained represent opportunities to invest spiritual gifts, those gifts of the Spirit listed in I Corinthians 12 and Romans 12 which are given to every true Christian without exception.

If this is so they would be opportunities earned, the right gained to exercise spiritual impact, spiritual power. How many Christians have discovered they have a spiritual gift only when they have seized an occasion to be of use to Christ? They have to decide to risk, to venture, for his name's sake. Feeling ill-equipped and clumsy at first, nevertheless, they went on doing what needed to be done and before long it was evident to all, and even to them, that they had a gift for the work, one of the gifts of the Spirit. Having found the spiritual gift they soon found great opportunity to employ it.

No risk, no gain—only loss

Inevitably Jesus moves to the climax of his story. One man yet remains to give his accounting:

> "He also who had received the one talent came forward, saying, 'Master, I knew you to be a hard man, reaping where you did not sow, and gathering where you did not winnow; so I was afraid, and I went and hid your talent in the ground. Here you have what is yours.' But his master answered him, 'You wicked and slothful servant! You knew that I reap where I have not sowed, and gather where I have not winnowed? Then you ought to have invested my money with the bankers, and at my coming I should have received what was my own with interest. So take the talent from him, and give it to him who has the ten talents. For to every one who has will more be given, and he will have abun-dance; but from him who has not, even what he has will be taken away. And cast the worthless servant

into the outer darkness; there men will weep and gnash their teeth.'"

At first we may be a bit bewildered by what seems an unduly harsh treatment of the man with one talent, who at least had a sense of responsibility to see that his master got back the money that he gave him without any loss. But the matter is put in proper perspective when we hear Jesus' words: "For to every one who has will more be given, and he will have abundance; but from him who has not, even what he has will be taken away." The basic purpose of life is growth, increase, return. To fail in this purpose is to be fundamentally unprofitable. All life grows, and if it does not it has already ceased to live and is no longer worth keeping. That is what Jesus means.

One big risk

This servant had gained nothing because he had risked nothing. There was no increase because there was no investment. He had one great (and long-continued) opportunity to risk himself on behalf of his master but he deliberately ignored it. The outcome of the story tells us the nature of that opportunity. It was the opportunity to give himself to God; the opportunity to be redeemed. That one supreme venture was a present possibility all through the time of his master's absence. But he had deliberately put it from himself, and rather early in the game. He had gone and hid it in the ground! When it was safely buried he could forget about it and go on about his own affairs. It was not there to make him uncomfortable by constantly reminding him of his master's expectations. But since he took no risk for Christ's sake he had also no spiritual influence, no impact for eternal good. His life counted for nothing; there was no spiritual power. It had all been lived for himself.

When the master returns the man has a little speech carefully prepared to justify it all. Evidently he had rehearsed it many

152

times. "You are," he says, "a basically unreasonable man. You expect profit without any labor on your part. You expect other people to do the dirty work while you get all the benefits, and if they should fail to satisfy your expectations you are quite ready to accuse them as thieves. So I was afraid to risk what you gave me, lest I should lose it and would have to face your wrath when you returned. But I have outwitted you. I have kept your talent safe for your return. Here is exactly what you gave me. You and I are even."

The master does not attempt to debate his character with the man. He takes him at his own appraisal of his master. "You knew that I reap where I have not sowed, and gather where I have not winnowed?" The editors of the text have done right in ending this statement with a question mark. The master is not agreeing with what the servant says, he is saying, in effect, "So that is your understanding of my character, is it? All right, then, out of your own mouth will I judge you. If that's what you thought of me, then you ought to have known that you couldn't possibly please me by failing to get some kind of gain. In that case, you could at least have put the money in the bank and I would have had some interest on it when I returned."

The phony revealed

Of course, the real problem is that the man had no intention of really being the servant he was pretending to be. The master's argument is: No matter what his opinion of his master was, whether true or distorted, as a true servant he should have acted in accord with what he knew his master would expect. But this the man refused to do. He had his own life to live and it was really nothing to him that a servant's fundamental task is to serve, not himself, but his lord. He was therefore a phony, a hypocrite, pretending to be what he was not.

In his selfish blindness what he did not realize was that his one chance to become genuine was to risk himself by venturing

153

with his master's talent. Had he done so, like the other two men, he would have gained. He would himself have been changed, for to venture *is* to be changed. To risk for Christ's sake is to find oneself altered, redeemed, reborn. That one talent is given to all who are drawn to follow Christ. They have the opportunity to risk themselves upon his word, to trust his redeeming grace, to rest their hope for eternity upon his work for them upon the cross. Other opportunities for risk will follow that, but without that one investment there is no true value to life.

As C. S. Lewis vividly puts it: "It may be a hard thing for an egg to become a bird; it is a jolly sight harder for it to learn to fly while it is still an egg. We are like eggs, today, and we either must be hatched, or go bad!"

Take a chance!

What is the final message of Jesus in telling this story? It is: Step out! Risk! Live dangerously! Take constant chances with your life and goods for his name's sake. Don't try to bottle up your life so as to hang on to it at all costs. If you do that you will surely lose it. But surrender yourself to his cause, again and again. That is the way to find life. That is the way to watch for his coming. Having risked yourself to become a Christian, now risk yourself again and again as opportunities arise. Live dangerously! Or that also could be written, love dangerously! To live for Christ is to love men with his love. And that is always a risk. It has been well written:

"To love at all is to be vulnerable. Love anything and your heart will certainly be wrung and possibly be broken. If you want to make sure of keeping it intact you must give your heart to no one, not even to an animal. Wrap it carefully around with hobbies and little luxuries, avoid all entanglements, lock it up

154

safe in the casket or the coffin of your selfishness. But in that casket—safe, dark, motionless, airless—it will change. It will not be broken, it will become unbreakable, impenetrable, irredeemable. The only place outside Heaven where you can be perfectly safe from all the dangers and perturbations of love is hell."*

———————

Prayer: Lord Jesus, have I ventured anything for you? Have I risked my life for your sake? or have I but transferred my ambition from the world of business or sport to the world of religion, still busy seeking self-aggrandizement, self-exaltation? Lord, teach me to risk, to abandon, to fling away what would minister only to myself. For your name's sake, Amen.

*Lewis, C.S., *The Four Loves*, Harcourt, Brace, World, Inc., New York. Used by permission.

13

The Unconscious Test
Matthew 25:31-46

This is the last chapter. If you've sneaked ahead to read it out of order because you can't wait to find out how it all ends, go ahead, read it! But come back to it again when you've finished the rest of the book. It will make much better sense to you then. But if you've stayed with us all the way you'll be anxious to know how Jesus ends this tremendous talk with his disciples on the Mount of Olives. He suddenly drops the use of parables and returns to a simple narrative. Unlike the household, the ten maidens, and the talents, the judgment of the sheep and goats with which he ends is not parable but fact. He introduces it with these words in verses 31-33:

> "When the Son of man comes in his glory, and all the angels with him, then he will sit on his glorious throne. Before him will be gathered all the nations, and he will separate them one from another as a shepherd separates the sheep from the goats, and he will place the sheep at his right hand, but the goats at the left."

It is hard for us to remember that these words were uttered by a Man standing in the gathering dusk on the Mount of Olives, in the midst of a tiny band of forsaken men, and looking out over a city where even at that moment his enemies were completing the plans for his arrest and execution. When Jesus uttered these words, by every human appearance he was defeated. The powers of darkness were triumphant, the shadow of the cross was falling across his pathway, the crowds that once had followed him had long since gone, his friends were fearful and powerless, and one of them was even then set to betray him. Yet as he surveyed the centuries he saw the light that was yet to come, and without uncertainty in his words, in that hour of triumphant evil and seeming human defeat, he declared, "When the Son of man comes in his glory . . . he will sit on his glorious throne. [And] before him will be gathered the nations."

A time for judgment

The mention of nations has proved confusing to some. They have thought of this as a judging of individuals on the basis of their national affiliation; i.e., each will be held accountable for the way his government behaved as a nation. But such is not the case. Those who appear before this judgment seat do not come as Englishmen or Americans or Chinese or Afghans. The Greek word translated "nations" is literally the word "Gentiles." This is, then, the judgment of the Gentiles, the non-Jewish peoples of earth. They are persons living on earth at the time of Christ's manifestation of his presence in power and great glory.

The purpose of the judgment is obviously to determine who shall enter the kingdom of God which the Son has come to establish. Through all the great discourses of Jesus in the gospels the evident passion of his heart is to see the will of God done on earth as it is in heaven. He will manifest himself in power for the very purpose of fulfilling those ancient dreams of the prophets—an earth that will be filled with the righteousness of God as the waters cover the sea. But only the righteous will be allowed to enter.

It is important to note, too, that it is a judgment of sheep and goats, not one of sheep and wolves! Jesus is not choosing between the obviously bad and the obviously good. There is here no division between the opponents of the gospel and the believers in it. That separation is to be made in the very hour of the appearing of Jesus in power and glory. As Paul tells us in II Thessalonians 1:9:

> "When the Lord Jesus is revealed from heaven with his mighty angels in flaming fire, inflicting vengeance upon those who do not know God and upon those who do not obey the gospel of our Lord Jesus. They shall suffer the punishment of eternal destruction and exclusion from the presence of the Lord and from the glory of his might."

But in the judgment of the sheep and the goats Jesus is distinguishing sharply among persons all of whom profess to be Christians and claim to belong to him as members of the family of God. It is the separation of the hypocrites from the real; of the false from the true.

Some commentators have felt there are three groups in this judgment scene: the sheep, the goats, and another group whom Jesus terms "my brethren" who are the point of testing at the judgment. These "brethren" would likely be the 144,000 Jewish believers who are closely identified with the Lord during the whole period of his presence behind the scenes. The Lord Jesus says to both the sheep and the goats, "'. . . as you did it [or did it not] to one of the least of these my brethren, you did it [or did it not] to me,'" It seems highly likely that there is this third group involved. Certainly during the Tribulation each of these 144,000 will be, as Jesus himself was in the days of his flesh, "despised and rejected of men." It will be a severe test of true love to show kindness toward them for they will be an object of furious hatred by the Lawless One and the authorities of earth in that day.

On the other hand, others feel that by "my brethren" the Lord is simply indicating any individual among the sheep or goats who is in need in the last days and to whom loving help is either extended or withheld. Whichever view is held it is evident that the principles of our Lord's judgment then are not different from the principles by which he judges men throughout the centuries. God acts, "as it was in the beginning, is now, and ever shall be, world without end, Amen." He will distinguish the hypocrites from among us today exactly on the same basis as he distinguished them then.

The real test

Let us now return to the scene our Lord describes, when he will do what no other figure in human history is capable of: dissolve all national distinctions, unite all the nations as one, and sit as the unchallenged Judge over all men:

> "Then the King will say to those at his right hand, 'Come, O blessed of my Father, inherit the kingdom prepared for you from the foundation of the world; for I was hungry and you gave me food, I was thirsty and you gave me drink, I was a stranger and you welcomed me, I was naked and you clothed me, I was sick and you visited me, I was in prison and you came to me.'"

The arresting thing about this is that Jesus is clearly saying that the ultimate mark of an authentic Christian is not his creed, or his faith, or his Bible knowledge, but the concern which he shows to those who are in need. The practical demonstration of love is the final proof. And note also that Jesus does not ask anyone to present his case or argue his cause. He asks no questions nor requests any evidence. He simply extends to this one group the invitation, "Come, O blessed of my Father, inherit the kingdom." Then he explains the basis of his choice. He has simply noted that when they had opportunity to help someone in need, they did it. Nothing more is required.

It is sobering to realize that Jesus identifies himself with those in need. If you help them, he says, you are really helping me; and if you ignore them you are ignoring me. He flings the cloak of relationship around them and calls them "my brethren." Speaking of the parable of the Good Samaritan, Dr. Helmut Thielicke says:

> "How easily we let a sentence like 'God is a God of love' pass over our lips. It even sounds a bit trite. But just let Jesus stand in front of us and look at us when we say the words and at once this pious little saying becomes an accusation. Then all of a sudden we hear it spoken by the beggar we shooed from our door yesterday, the servant-girl we dismissed, perhaps because she was going to have a baby, the neighbor whose name has recently been dragged through the newspapers because of some disgraceful affair, whom we let know that we always walk the straight and narrow path. Suddenly we hear them all speaking it, because this saying has something to do with all of them, not only with the God who dwells above the clouds, for in them the eyes of the Lord himself are gazing at us."*

The sheep who inherit the kingdom are those who have responded to these needs in love, concern, and ministry. They have probably done so at considerable cost or risk to them-

*How the World Began, Fortress Press, Philadelphia. Used by permission.

selves. But no matter, they did what they could. With the goats it is the opposite story:

> "Then he will say to those at his left hand, 'Depart from me, you cursed, into the eternal fire prepared for the devil and his angels; for I was hungry and you gave me no food, I was thirsty and you gave me no drink, I was a stranger and you did not welcome me, naked and you did not clothe me, sick and in prison and you did not visit me.'"

The seriousness of this matter of helping the needy is seen in the severity of the Lord's words here. "Depart from me you cursed, into the eternal fire prepared for the devil and his angels." And let us remember that these are people who honestly think they are sheep! They can point with pride to a moment when they made a profession of belief, they are, perhaps, dogmatic about a creed and are church members in good standing, but by their lack of response to the pleas for help that come to them from every side they stand revealed as goats—false sheep—who never were sheep at all.

What a surprise!

The reaction of both the sheep and the goats to the Lord's words is one of stunned surprise. They are completely taken aback by what he says. It is clearly evident that both groups expected a different basis of judgment. As they were being divided into one group or another they doubtless felt they knew the reason for the choice. Surely the sheep would feel that the basis was that of faith. There would be ringing in their ears all the great and marvelous words of Scripture declaring that justification before God is by faith alone. Can't you see them waiting to come before the King, each one nervously reviewing his testimony, trying to recall the exact wording of the great promises on

161

which he would rest all his hopes for this moment?

But the strange thing is, not one is ever given the chance to say a word. The issue is already settled. Each person is simply told to which group he belongs.

> "Then the righteous will answer him, 'Lord, when did we see thee hungry and feed thee, or thirsty and give thee drink? And when did we see thee a stranger and welcome thee, or naked and clothe thee? And when did we see thee sick or in prison and visit thee?'"

But of course the issue really *is* one of faith. The sheep are asked to take their place on the right hand of the throne because all through their lives their genuine faith has been producing its inevitable fruit of good works. Unthinkingly, unconsciously, born of love for Jesus Christ, they have been responding to the pleas and needs of those about them. They kept no records, they expected no praise. For them it has been a glad privilege. They were unaware they were doing anything unusual, but found a real delight in meeting the needs of others. There was no hardship involved to them. They felt it was a continuing joy to be permitted to minister in Christ's name. But not one deed performed in that way has ever escaped the eye of their watching Lord. There is no need for him to examine them. They had laid up abundant treasure in heaven.

But the goats are equally surprised. They, too, are caught off guard by this basis of judgment:

> "Then they also will answer, 'Lord, when did we see thee hungry or thirsty or a stranger or naked or sick or in prison, and did not minister to thee?'"

Yet they may have guessed even more closely than the sheep the true basis for judgment. Very likely they are sure that

162

it is good works. They know that God is interested in the poor, the down-trodden, the oppressed, and they are all ready for him. Already they have been making long mental lists of the many times they have ministered to those in need about them. They can recall detailed descriptions of what they did. They can total up large sums of money given, complete with income tax receipts. No doubt the amount of money so expended is terribly impressive, for as someone has remarked, it takes a great deal of philanthropy to deodorize a fortune! They have even put in long hours working for charity, fighting for racial equality, or protesting substandard housing.

To these self-justifying persons the King replies: "Truly, I say to you, as you did it not to one of the least of these, you did it not to me."

Good works that aren't good

They are even more surprised than the sheep at the Lord's words. It was good deeds of the very type he describes that they were depending upon for acceptance in this hour. They are at a total loss to understand his rejection. But they have forgotten what Jesus says in the Sermon on the Mount. There he is careful to tell us that deeds done "to be seen by men" already have their reward. Even if the deeds are not publicly known, if they are done for private satisfaction they are in the same category. "Let not your left hand know what your right hand does," he says. That is, do not even take note of what you do yourself; do not even privately pat yourself on the back.

It is the times which they have forgotten that he uses for judgment, and not the times they remember. It is the times they looked the other way when some begging hand reached out. The times they were busy with other demands when word came of the sick and the dying. The times when they refused, through shame or pride, to visit some poor wretch in prison lest they be associated with him. Their eyes were averted as they walked around the stricken man lying by the wayside. They turned deaf ears to pleas when they could have helped. But these incidents have long been forgotten. They are quite honest when they say in astonishment, "Lord, when?"

But this is false Christianity, no matter how much it may be dressed in evangelical clothes. Perhaps nothing can describe it better than this prayer, written by Richard Woike. He calls it "A Prayer to Avoid," but we might well term it, "The Prayer of a Goat."

"0 thou pleasant, comfortable, kindly, good-natured God: How glad I am that I can look forward, with a reasonable degree of certainty, to another ordinary day. Keep me today from anything that taxes my faith, from discomfort, from unnecessary strain, from unusual problems, especially those involving sickness or death, or the necessity of extending financial aid to relatives and friends.

"Dear Lord, grant that nothing may occur which will disturb my satisfaction with the way I am, and the things I say, and the thoughts I think, the acts I do, or the many deeds I leave undone. Give me this day, in addition to my daily bread, the butter, meats, and sweetmeats that are my necessary diet, and let me not be troubled by qualms of conscience concerning the amount of time and money I spend on food and clothing, pastimes, good and bad, and those pursuits which, while not of spiritual value, are the accepted hallmark of the normal citizen of this enlightened community in this enlightened age.

"About the future and the darkening trend of things, keep me from thoughtfulness. Events rush on, the world travails. Can screaming headlines prove thy hand's at work this very moment, bringing nearer that fateful cry, 'Behold! He comes!'? O Lord,

164

such disconcerting thoughts! Keep me from worrying about such things, and guide me safely to and from my office and my home. Amen."*

How man judges; how God judges

Nothing reveals more sharply the radical difference between God's judging and man's than this story of the sheep and the goats. Even our treasured "good deeds" are shown up for what they are in the searching light from this throne of glory. Good deeds that are not the unconscious, automatic response of a heart indwelt by Jesus Christ are not truly "good" deeds. They are planned deeds, contrived, carefully performed for the public eye, or if in private, done in the hope that they will purchase some merit or favor before God.

But God's judgments take note only of the unconscious moments of our lives, the times when we are off guard, when we are unaware. It is then that we truly reveal ourselves. The test comes, not in our remembered actions, but in our unconscious reactions, our instinctive, unplanned responses.

This was borne sharply to my mind some time ago when, in the company of a number of friends, I attended a public concert in a large city. The officials of both the city and state were in attendance and a great crowd had jammed into a small open-air square. The officials were seated in front row chairs on a small platform. Among the various performers that night was a young starlet from Hollywood. She was dressed in a gownless evening strap and in this revealing attire came to the microphone to sing. She did several swinging numbers, swaying with her hips and snapping her fingers. As she sang I happened to turn to note the reaction of the mayor of the city, seated on the front row.

*Used by permission.

Evidently he had lost himself in the performance, for his guard was down. His eyes were agleam with lechery, his mouth had dropped partly open, and he was fairly drooling. I saw also the governor of the state, seated a few chairs away, who was eyeing the mayor with a stern look of disapproval. While I watched, the governor caught the mayor's eye. Immediately he reddened, shifted uneasily in his chair, closed his mouth, sat straight up, and looked out over the audience. The governor's glance had said to him, in the most eloquent silence I have ever heard, "Shape up, man, you're in public!" Though the mayor was the soul of propriety the rest of the evening, in one unconscious moment reality had shown through.

The life that wins

If we are not going to be tested by the times when we are alert and on guard, but God is "unfair" enough to catch us when we are simply responding to what we are, then what we are must be what he demands. There is only one life that is sufficient for that kind of demand. Only one life is capable of responding instantaneously with unselfish love to the needs of others. That is the life of Jesus Christ. If we have not received him into our hearts we do not have that life. If we have received him we need to make ourselves available to him. We should be willing moment by moment to reach out to others in the strength and love which he will impart to us as soon as we begin to obey. This alone is the life that can meet the test.

The one great word—WATCH!

Now the discourse is ended. We have heard the greatest prophet who ever lived outline for us the history of the future. It has been a fascinating experience, containing many surprising and unexpected revelations. If we had never read this discourse before we could not possibly have guessed what the outcome of history will be. But now that we know, what shall we do about it?

There can be only one answer to that. We must do what our Lord says. We must obey the command he repeats again and again. Watch! Keep alert! Watch! We have learned now what that means. It means three specific and definite things:

- **It means we are to help one another feed upon the living Lord Jesus, as revealed in the written Word of God. We must study the Book.**
- **It means we must walk in the Spirit, depending not upon our human resources and weapons, but upon the power of an indwelling Spirit who is God himself, at work in us.**
- **It means we must live dangerously, venturing ourselves for Christ's sake. We must keep thrusting out in his name, buying up every opportunity to meet those around us at the point of their need.**

This, and this alone, is watching. Nothing can take its place. Therefore, "Watch at all times, praying that you may have strength to escape all these things that will take place, and to stand before the Son of man" (Luke 21:36).

Prayer: Holy Father, how easy it is to be orthodox in word and unorthodox in deed, to be compassionate in a meeting and selfish and cruel at home. But thank you for the cleansing grace so freely available in the Lord Jesus. Teach us how to live by him so that all we do and say is a manifestation of his life at work in us. In Jesus' name, Amen.